American Doughboys in the First World War

Robert J Mueller

A Fields of War Visitor's Guide to Historic Sites

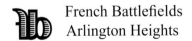

French Battlefields
Arlington Heights

French Battlefields
PO Box 4808
Buffalo Grove, Illinois 60089-4808
Email: contact@frenchbattlefields.com
Web address: http://www.frenchbattlefields.com

Copyright 2018 by Robert J Mueller
All rights reserved
Cover design by Vince Martinez
First Edition
Manufactured in the United States
Library of Congress Control Number: 2018909112
ISBN-13: 978-0-9823677-7-3; ISBN-10: 0-9823677-7-5
Unless otherwise indicated, all photographs and illustrations are the property of the
author. No part of this book may be reproduced or transmitted without the written
permission of the publisher.

Cover photographs:
Reflecting Pool and Chapel in Meuse-Argonne American Cemetery
Headquarters Company, 23rd Regiment, 2nd Division firing during the American
advance in the St-Mihiel Salient (NARA);
Armor of Company C, 327th Tank Battalion near Seicheprey on 12 September 1918
(NARA);
American observer looks east from Montfaucon toward Bois de Septsarges (NARA)

Abbreviations used for photographs:
NARA: National Archives and Records Administration
USAMHI: Unites States Army Military History Institute
ABMC: American Battle Monuments Commission

Dedicated to:
Those who served

Contents

Introduction

To the people of France, 'The War' refers not to the Second World War as it would for most Americans, but to The Great War of 1914 – 1918. Those four years of static conflict ravaged the villages and countryside of northern France and forced hardship upon all its citizens, nearly destroying the entire country. The war years witnessed the death or physical maiming of 27 percent of the male population between 18 and 27 years of age, not including those mentally and emotionally shattered by their war experiences. A generation of marriageable women went without husbands, young children without fathers, and parents without sons.

The Treaty of Versailles rewrote the map of Europe and the Middle East ,creating new countries frequently along arbitrary borders and ignoring ethnic rivalries. One hundred years later those rivalries continue to roil the Balkans, create tension between the European Union and Russia, and stir religious conflict between Arab nations and their Persian and Israeli neighbors. The issues of the First World War are with us to this day.

The war also thrust a new global power onto the world stage. Although conflicted between supporting allies and a strong desire to avoid foreign entanglements, the United States of America reluctantly entered what many of its citizens believed to be a solely European conflict.

Nearly forgotten after the suffering of the Great Depression and the destruction of the Second World War, American battlefields and memorials of the First World War stand in proud remembrance of the men who left their towns and farms to fight for a cause. The people of France continue to revere and protect the sites of this great conflict and the symbols that honor the men who fought there. So should we.

American Military Cemeteries

Overseas American military cemeteries are administered by the American Battle Monument Commission (ABMC), an agency of the executive branch of the federal government. Each cemetery is administered by an on-site superintendent. American representatives are always on duty in the visitor's center to assist in locating grave sites or to provide information on the cemetery. Information regarding ABMC cemeteries or the 218,000 service personal buried in them can be found at https://www.abmc.gov. All American military cemeteries in Europe are open every day from 09:00 to 17:00, except 25 December and 1 January. Special commemorations of American Memorial Day are held every year on the fourth Monday in May and are worth attending. The cemetery land has been granted to the people of the United States by the people of France in gratitude and in perpetuity for use as a military cemetery.

How to Use this Book

This guide brings battlefield visitors to specific sites of important battlefield events, describes what happened there, and offers opportunities to view commemorations, visit museums, or inspect surviving relics of the battle. Each battlefield description begins with a brief summary of the precipitating military events. A Fact Box summarizes key information and a detailed Battlefield Map assists in following the action and locating selected sites. The Battle section describes each commander's objectives and troop movements. The Aftermath section notes results of the fighting and significant events which occurred after the engagement. The major section of each battle is devoted to the Battlefield Tour. Each tour starts at an easy to locate town. Clear driving instructions, highlighted in boxes for easy reading, are designed to bring a visitor to various positions of importance on the battlefield. A brief description of the site highlights individual contributions to the battles outcome. Footnotes provide insights into individual soldiers' post-war lives.

Tourist offices can provide helpful information regarding accommodations, cultural and historic sites, walking or cycling routes, and hours of operation for museums. The Michelin Green Guide is highly recommended for its presentation of general tourist information. It makes an excellent accompaniment to this book and offers general touring advice in addition to listing historic and cultural locations, market days, festivals, and public holidays.

Twenty-four hour military time is in use in Europe; therefore operational hours in this book are so presented. Outside of the major French metropolitan areas, tourist offices, many museums, most retail shops, and all banks honor the French custom of closing during midday. Weekday and Saturday morning hours are frequently restricted to 9:00 to 12:00 and 14:00 to 17:00. On Sundays and public holidays, almost all establishments are closed, with many restaurants closing after the noon meal. Sites open on weekends are frequently closed on Mondays or Tuesdays. Some variations exist, especially later closing hours during the summer tourist season. Few museums are handicap accessible; those that so advertise are indicated.

Local citizens are remarkably tolerant of battlefield visitors; however private property should be respected and never accessed without owner's permission. Crops are the farmer's livelihood and trampling planted fields should be avoided, although a field boundary often provides a useful walk path. Forests, signed chasse privé or chasse gardé are private and may be the scene of the shooting season from August to March; care should be exercised. Finally, an additional word of caution: abandoned bunkers or off-trail battlefield terrain frequently retain dangerous spikes, barbed wire, or even unexploded ordinance. Utmost caution must be exercised and independent exploration is discouraged.

The information contained herein is believed to be accurate at the time of printing, but museum hours are notoriously subject to change. If access to a certain site is of paramount importance, it is best to contact it in advance. Each year, roadways are improved or re-routed and intersections reconstructed. Therefore, up-to-date road maps or GPS navigators are a necessity. Geographic coordinates (latitude, longitude), which can be entered into GPS navigators, are given for each location allowing visitors to select those sites of individual interest or to alter the order of visitation. For those unable or unwilling to provide their own transportation, a few tour companies offer a reasonable alternative. The tour routes described may pass many other commemorations erected on French or British battlefields of the Great War. They frequently make interesting viewing but are considered outside the scope of this work.

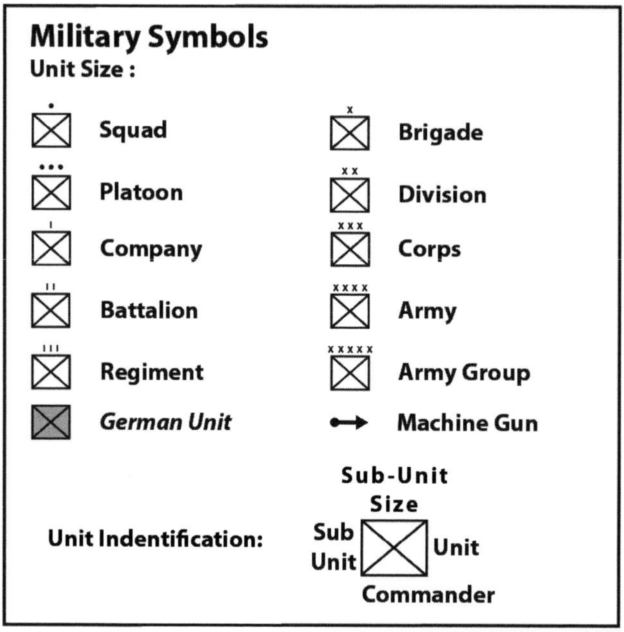

Military Symbols
Unit Size :

⊠ **Squad**

⊠ **Platoon**

⊠ **Company**

⊠ **Battalion**

⊠ **Regiment**

⊠ *German Unit*

⊠ **Brigade**

⊠ **Division**

⊠ **Corps**

⊠ **Army**

⊠ **Army Group**

⬌ **Machine Gun**

Unit Indentification:

Sub-Unit Size

Sub Unit ⊠ Unit

Commander

The First World War

Toward the end of the 19th century and during the first years of the 20th century, the great military powers of Europe established a system of mutual defense alliances that attempted to retain a balance of power in Europe. In the face of rising German economic and military power resulting from its unification and victory in the Franco-Prussian War of 1870/71, France, Britain, and Russia formed the Triple Entente in 1894 to counterbalance the Triple Alliance formed by Germany, Austria-Hungary, and Italy in 1882. After the war started, Italy declared its neutrality, then joined the Triple Entente while Bulgaria and the Ottoman Empire joined the Germanic countries in an alliance known as the Central Powers.

On 28 June 1914, Archduke Franz Ferdinand, heir to the throne of Austria-Hungary, and his wife Duchess Sophie were assassinated by Serbian nationalist Gavrilo Princip[1] in Sarajevo, the capital of the Austro-Hungarian province of Bosnia and Herzegovina.

After a month of Serbia denying involvement and refusing Austria's demands for the assassin's co-conspirators, Austria-Hungary declared war on Serbia. Mutual defense protocols were immediately triggered and within eight days, Russia mobilized its armed forces (29 July); Germany declared war on Russia while France and Belgium mobilized their Armies (1 August); Germany declared war on France and invaded neutral Belgium (3 August); Great Britain declared war on Germany (4 August); and Austria declared war on Russia (6 August). Finally, on 12 August, France and Great Britain declared war on Austria-Hungary. The great European conflict had begun.

German strategic plans relied heavily on execution of the 1905 Schlieffen Plan, which called for the rapid defeat of French and Belgian armies before slow-to-mobilize Russia could transport its huge army to Germany's eastern borders. During the first months of the war, the rapid assault toward Paris occupied Luxembourg, most of Belgium, and large areas of France's industrialized northern provinces, but failed to overcome French and British resistance. Eventually, a battle line developed from the North Sea to the Swiss border which became known as the Western Front.

Trenches were dug, fortified, attacked, lost, and recaptured in a never ending cycle of death and destruction. Poison gas drifted across the landscape in great yellow clouds, killing everything in its path. For the frontline troops, life took on a surreal existence of living underground, navigating vast seas of mud, and witnessing the death or maiming of one's comrades.

By autumn of 1917 this hopeless warfare had been raging for three years, but the Western Front had moved very little since the first months of war. Both sides exhausted themselves in horrific battles at Ypres, Somme, Verdun, and Passchendaele which produced no strategic gains for either side at the cost of over three million casualties.

---

1   Gavrilo Princip, 19 years old, was a member of the Young Bosnia revolutionary movement and one of a group of assassins organized and armed by the Black Hand, a secret military society formed by officers of the Army of the Kingdom of Serbia. Princip was apprehended and the young assassin received the maximum sentence of twenty years in prison, avoiding the death penalty due to his age. Held in harsh conditions which worsened during the war, he contracted tuberculosis and died on 28 April 1918.

American Troops Enter the War

For the first three years of the First World War America avoided what it considered to be a European conflict. President Woodrow Wilson won re-election in 1916 on the campaign slogan 'He kept us out of war.' However, British propaganda slowly turned American public opinion against the Central Powers.

On 1 February 1917 Germany resumed unrestricted submarine warfare, attempting to starve the British population into capitulation just as the British blockade of German North Sea ports starved civilians in Germany. German submarines attacked all merchant shipping, including that of neutral countries, in the seas around the British Isles. By 21 March, seven American merchant ships had been sunk with the loss of thirty-five seamen. On 2 April 1917 President Wilson asked Congress for a declaration of war and he received it four days later.

America however, was not prepared for war, having only a small army of 300,000 men (including the National Guard) and very little in the way of artillery, airplanes, leadership, or tactical skills. The War Department federalized the states' National Guard units to quickly augment the small standing army. Then-major Douglas MacArthur[2] suggested and received agreement that the first National Guard division be organized from units of

President Woodrow Wilson requests a Declaration of War from the US Congress. (NARA)

different states, to avoid the appearance of favoritism toward any particular state. This formation became the 42nd 'Rainbow' Division with now-promoted Colonel MacArthur as its chief of staff.

President Wilson selected General John J 'Black Jack' Pershing[3] to head the American Expeditionary Force. The regular army's 1st Division, later nicknamed 'The

---

2   General Douglas MacArthur became one of America's most honored, flamboyant, and controversial generals in its history. His aggressiveness in the First World War earned two Distinguished Service Crosses and seven Silver Stars. He commanded the Army of the Philippines when the Japanese launched America into the Second World War with their attacks of 7 December 1941. He is famously remembered for his promise 'I shall return' upon being ordered to evacuate the islands. MacArthur accepted the Japanese surrender in Tokyo Bay on 2 September 1945. In 1951 during the Korean War, he was unceremoniously relieved by President Harry Truman for insubordination when he was exposed as conducting private diplomatic conversations that were contrary to American policy.

3   In 1898, Major Pershing, as a regimental officer with the famous 10th Cavalry Regiment, participated in the assault on the San Juan Heights in Cuba. He garnered the nickname 'Black Jack' for comparing the high level of professionalism and discipline of the black 'Buffalo Soldiers' with other troops.

Big Red One,' were the first America troops to land in St-Nazaire, France on 26 June 1917. The buildup of American forces was slow, and for the most part the troops were supplied weapons and equipment by the French and British including the distinctive British 'Tommy' helmet.

Almost immediately conflict erupted among the Allied High Command. British and French commanders saw Americans as ready cannon folder to refill decimated battalions in their armies. Pershing stoutly refused. He declared that Americans would fight in American units under American officers and American NCOs. However, the green American troops were untrained, ill-equipped, and far from ready for the difficulties of fighting in Western Front trenches. Therefore, its battalions of infantry were assigned for training under French tutelage mainly in southern sectors of the Western Front.

On 21 October, four months after their arrival in France, the first American units were assigned to Allied trenches in the Lunéville sector near Nancy, France for training. The 16th Regiment held positions near Bathelémont, a small farming community amid rolling hills near the then French-German border.

On 2 November 1917, chilled by cold and fog, the regiment's Company F entered frontline trenches. At 03:30, a violent bombardment fell on Artois Hill during German Operation JAKOBSBRUNNEN to capture American soldiers for interrogation. A box barrage isolated a section of the frontline trenches and covered the movement of 250 Bavarian troops. American defenders engaged in hand-to-hand combat illuminated only by the flash of exploding artillery shells. The fighting was over in 24 minutes as the Bavarians returned to their lines

Marshal Ferdinand Foch, commander-in-chief of Allied Forces, and General John J Pershing, the commander-in-chief of American Expeditionary Forces. (USAMHI)

with eleven prisoners and left the bodies of James Bethel Gresham, a 24-year-old corporal from Evansville, Indiana, Private Thomas Enright, a 34-year-old son of Irish immigrants from Pittsburgh, Pennsylvania, and Private Merle Hay, a farm boy from Glidden, Iowa. Hay and Gresham were killed in the initial attack, after not recognizing the Germans soldiers in the dark; Enright was killed as he resisted being taken captive. They were the first American soldiers killed in the First World War. They would not be the last. Although the men were originally entombed on a hill overlooking the village, all three bodies were returned to the United States after the war.

French citizens erected a memorial in front of the old church in Bathelémont in November 1918 to commemorate the three dead American soldiers. Nazi occupation forces destroyed the memorial in October 1940 because the original inscription referred to Germans as 'The Scourge of Humanity.' A rebuilt memorial now stands at the entrance to the Bathelémont-lès-Bauzemont Cemetery, 350 meters west of the village center. Its inscription states, 'Here on Lorraine soil, rest the first three American soldiers killed by the enemy.' Beside the memorial are the remains of the original monument. [4] (48.690496, 6.519474)

Kaiserschlacht

In late 1917, catastrophe befell the Allies. The Russian Army, which had suffered some of the worst casualty rates of the war amid shortages of clothing, boots, and weapons, rebelled. The Czar's government fell to eventually be replaced by Vladimir Lenin's Communist People's Government. The Bolsheviks immediately sued for peace with Germany. The Treaty of Brest-Litovsk was signed on 3 March 1918, freeing two million German troops to be transferred from the Eastern Front to fight against the Allies in the west.

As winter turned into spring in 1918, American troops were arriving in France by the thousands and would soon redress the temporary German manpower advantage. Quartermaster-General Erich Ludendorff [5] knew that he had a limited time frame within which to act. The *Kaiserschlacht* or 'Emperor's Battle' involved a series of massive assaults from Ypres to Reims with the hope that they would split the French and British armies and cause the French to sue for peace. German forces utilized lightly equipped troops in new 'stormtrooper' tactics that ended the static trench warfare of the past three years. On 21 March 1918, the first of these efforts struck along a 90-km front from Arras to La Fère. Using ten thousand guns, Ludendorff's artillery fired nearly as many shells in five hours as the British had in the

Generalfeldmarschall Paul von Hindenburg, Kaiser Wilhelm II, and Quartermaster-General Erich Ludendorf pose at GHQ in January 1917. Note: the Kaiser hid his disabled left arm. (NARA)

---

4   The location is described only because of its historical significance. Unfortunately it is remote from other American battlefields and consists only of the relocated memorial.

5   General Erich Ludendorff was the son of a Prussian Junker family and entered a distinguished military academy at an early age. He successfully led Eastern Front actions against Russia with victories at the Battles of Tannenberg and the Masurian Lakes. In 1916 Ludendorff was promoted to General der Infanterie and became Paul von Hindenburg's chief of staff with the title of First Quartermaster-General.

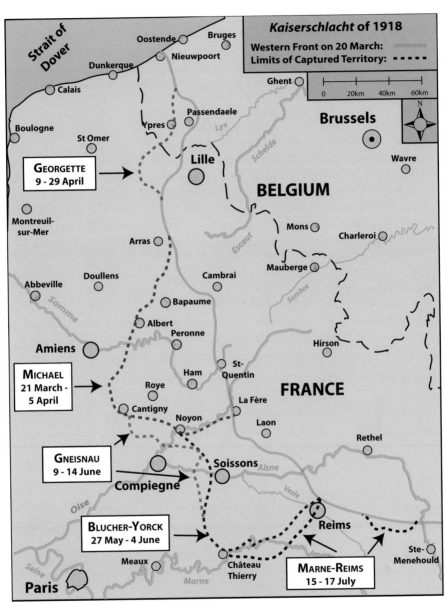

Kaiserschlacht Offensives

week before their massive Somme Offensive of 1916. The barrage preceded an attack from forty infantry divisions. After the first two hours, forty-seven British battalions ceased to exist as operational units. The unprecedented ferocity of the attack ruptured the British line and began to drive apart the British Third and Fifth Armies. For the next two weeks, wave upon wave of German infantry drove British units inexorably back across the Somme battlefield until the line was finally stabilized on 4 April, just kilometers east of the critical transportation center of Amiens.

Losses to the Allies were catastrophic, numbering over 177,000 British and 77,000 French. Although the German army had recovered more territory in a thirteen-day period than the Allies had in three years of warfare, the 239,000 men lost were irreplaceable. Worse still, they had captured no strategic ground and their exhausted men and equipment were well beyond the range of their supply infrastructure.

Battle of Cantigny
28 May 1918

During the emergency created by the German offensive, General Pershing placed all American combat troops at the disposal of Allied commander général Ferdinand Foch. In May, the American 1st Division was sent west of Montdidier under command of X Corps, French First Army. The German-held village of Cantigny lay on high ground in a salient in the front lines. On 28 May 1918, the first offensive action by the newly created First American Army was to capture and hold the French village.

OBJECTIVE	To capture and hold the high ground around the village
FORCES	
AMERICAN:	28th Regiment (Colonel Hansen Ely), 1st Division (Major General Robert Lee Bullard)
GERMAN:	Infantry Regiments Nr 271 and Nr 272, 82nd Reserve Division (Generalleutnant Baron von St Ange)
RESULT	The village was captured and held against German counterattack.
CASUALTIES	
AMERICAN:	199 killed; 668 wounded or missing
GERMAN:	1,400 killed or wounded; 250 taken prisoner
LOCATION	Compiègne is 85 km northeast of Paris; Cantigny is 40 km northwest of Compiègne

Battle

At 06:40, American troops went over the top of the frontline trenches behind a creeping artillery barrage and supported by French artillery, mortars, machine gunners, and flamethrowers. Three battalions abreast, each with one company in reserve, moved from west of the village. The regiment's 2nd Battalion, with two companies of the 18th Regiment in reserve and accompanied by twelve

German soldier flees before a French flamethrower amid the ruins of Cantigny. NARA

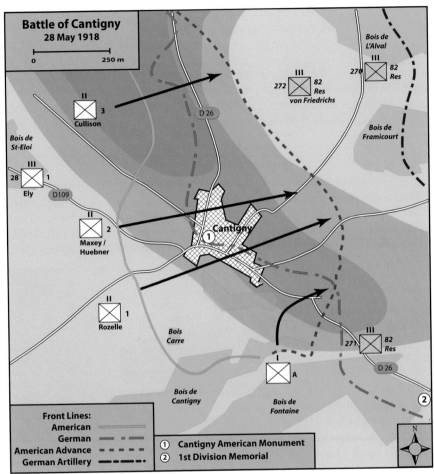

Battle of Cantigny

Schneider tanks from the French 5th Tank Battalion, was assigned to occupy the village. Eager American infantrymen rushed ahead of their tank support, closing with their own barrage. Upon entering the village, they fought from house to house, clearing out the deep, shell-proof cellars in the village's old stone houses. Bayonet duels paired American against German. By noon, Cantigny was in American hands. However, the positions of the enemy artillery in forests to the northeast were not taken, and German shells fell among the Americans before they had dug shelters. A heavy artillery barrage preceded the first large-scale counterattack at 17:10. Captain Clarence Huebner assumed command of the 2nd Battalion, after Lieutenant Colonel Robert Maxey was seriously wounded and later died.[6] Huebner established a strongpoint and

---

6   Lieutenant Colonel Robert Maxey received the Distinguished Service Cross posthumously for continuing to guide his command despite being mortally wounded. Maxey, 45 years old, is buried in the United States Military Academy Post Cemetery.

repelled repeated German attempts to penetrate back into the village.[7] The attacks continued for 72 hours, but the Americans held the town.

Aftermath

Capture of the high ground at Cantigny disrupted German plans for a resumption of Operation MICHAEL. Although not a significant battle compared to the massive offensives earlier in the war, the Battle of Cantigny was the first proof that American soldiers could fight and win on a First World War battlefield. Much bigger tests were to come.

Battlefield Tour

The battlefield tour focuses upon the **Cantigny American Monument** which commemorates the engagement in an attractive park in the center of the small village. A white stone shaft mounted upon an elevated platform with sculpted American Eagles on each of its four corners carries a description of the events. The quiet surroundings now give no hint of the bitter hand-to-hand fighting which took place over this ground 100 years ago. On the 90th anniversary of the battle, the Robert R McCormick Foundation[8] unveiled a statue depicting a doughboy charging with raised rifle and bayonet. The statue bears the shield of the Black Lion of Picardy; an emblem that the 28th Regiment adopted after the battle and which it retains to this day. The street that runs beside the park has been renamed rue 1st Division USA. (49.663403, 2.491253)

Cantigny American Monument

At the edge of town southeast toward St-Médard (D26), one of the ten 1st Division memorials scattered across the battlefields of Europe records the names of the 199 men killed in the local fighting. The modest remembrance consists of a small concrete shaft surmounted by a carved stone eagle. (49.659268, 2.501518)

---

7   Clarence Ralph Huebner, a farm boy from Bushton, Kansas, spent almost seven years advancing from private to sergeant in the infantry. Huebner received a regular commission in November 1916. He was twice decorated with the Distinguished Service Cross for his actions at Cantigny and later at Soissons. Major General Clarence Ralph Huebner commanded the US 1st Infantry Division during the Omaha Beach landings 26 years later. He led the division through battles in Normandy and into the Hürtgen Forest. Promoted to lieutenant general, he commanded V Corps across the Rhine and into Germany. After the war, he served as military governor of the American Zone in Germany. Huebner died in 1972 at age 83 and is buried in Arlington National Cemetery.

8   Colonel Robert R McCormick commanded the 1st Battalion, 5th Field Artillery Regiment during the battle. Col McCormick was co-editor, publisher, and later owner of the Chicago Tribune newspaper and his estate established the Cantigny Park and Museum in Wheaton, Illinois to commemorate the 1st Infantry Division.

Battle of Belleau Wood
6 to 25 June 1918

After the failed attempt to capture Amiens during Operation MICHAEL, Ludendorff attacked British positions in Flanders, threatening the vital channel ports of Boulogne-sur-Mer and Calais. Although Operation GEORGETTE failed to achieve these objectives, it did force the British Second Army to abandon the Passchendaele salient that had cost it so many lives to capture the previous year. The Germans also pushed the French off strategic Mount Kemmel.

Ludendorff then turned his attention to the Chemin des Dames battlefield. On 27 May, he launched Operation BLÜCHER-YORCK with twenty-seven divisions of the German Seventh Army against the French Sixth Army. Originally intended as a feint, the effort was so successful in overrunning five recuperating French and British divisions and occupying positions on the Marne River only 90 km from Paris that Ludendorff decided to continue the offensive. The force of the attack panicked some French units and with the road to Paris essentially open, général Philippe Pétain, newly appointed Commander-in-Chief of the French Army, petitioned General Pershing for help. The only combat-ready troops Pershing could offer were the American 2nd and 3rd Divisions. Pershing immediately ordered both units to proceed toward Château-Thierry.

The 2nd Division was a hybrid unit composed of a brigade of regular army soldiers and a brigade of American Marines. On 1 June, as the Marines approached the Bois de Belleau, they found the French retreating. A French officer suggested that the Marines do the same. Captain Lloyd Williams, commander of the 51st Company, 5th Marine Regiment,

German patrol mopping up a village between the Marne and Aisne Rivers, Spring 1918. NARA

refused replying, 'Retreat, Hell! We just got here.' By 2 June, the Marines were in position west of Château-Thierry, where it became the only operational unit between the Germans and Paris while dispirited French troops passed through its line seeking safety to the rear.[9]

---

9   Captain Lloyd Williams, 31 years old, would get no further. He was killed ten days later. Williams, gassed and injured by shrapnel, lay wounded on the battlefield. He told the approaching medics 'Don't bother with me. Take care of my good men.' Williams later died from a shell explosion as he was being evacuated. Williams was posthumously awarded the Distinguished Service Cross and promoted to major. The US Marine Corps' 2nd Battalion, 5th Regiment adopted the motto: 'Retreat, Hell!' which it uses to this day.

By early June, Ludendorff's logistical problems precluded a defense of the salient created by the sudden German advance. French and American commanders decided to recapture what they thought was a lightly-defended Bois de Belleau. As part of a massive French counterattack against the exhausted Germans, the 2nd Division was assigned to attack the forested hilltop and the small villages of Bouresches and Vaux to protect the right flank of the neighboring French 167th Division.

The Bois de Belleau was once the hunting preserve of the Château de Belleau, which was in the village of the same name one kilometer to its north. The wood was not as lightly defended as had been assumed. The hardwood forest sheltered 1,169 Prussian troops amidst outcroppings of huge rock formations which offered protection from artillery shelling and provided ideal positions for the placement of machine guns and mortars. The forest held three defensive trench lines. The first trench along the southern edge held fifteen Maxim machine guns with interlocking fields of fire positioned behind huge boulders and downed trees; the second trench ran east to west through the center of the forest; the third and strongest trench line ran along the northern edge of the wood and was fortified by artillery units positioned behind Torcy-en-Valois.

OBJECTIVE	To eliminate a German salient
FORCES	
AMERICAN:	4th Marine Brigade (Brigadier General James Harbord)
GERMAN:	Infantry Regiment Nr 461, 237th Division (Major Josef Bischoff)
RESULT	Bois de Belleau was captured after suffering heavy casualties.
CASUALTIES	
AMERICAN:	1,811 killed, 7,966 wounded or missing
GERMAN:	Unknown killed and wounded; 1,600 taken prisoner
LOCATION	Château-Thierry is 90 km northeast of Paris; Belleau Wood is 11 km west of Château-Thierry

Battle

At 05:00 on 6 June, Companies 49 and 67, 1st Battalion, 5th Marine Regiment, commanded by Major Julius Turrill, followed an American and French artillery barrage to attack Hill 142. Supported by 8th and 23rd Machine Gun Companies, 486 Marines waded 300 meters through poppy-flecked, waist-high wheat filling the gentle slope up to the pine-covered crest. The ridge was defended by three companies of Prussian troops. The Marines were met with a burst of shrapnel but kept advancing in four waves. Despite the intense enemy fire, they continued forward yelling curses and bayoneting German machine gun teams as they went. The 67th Company had most of their officers wounded, when Corporal Prentice Geer took charge to lead assaults against enemy guns. Company 49 fared better also crossing the wheat field but succeeded in driving the enemy up and over the ridge before stopping to consolidate. [10]

---

10   Corporal Prentice S Geer, from St Paul, Minnesota, was awarded the Distinguished Service Cross for his extraordinary heroism. Geer remained in the Marine Corps rising to the rank of brigadier general. He died at age 71 and is buried in Fort Rosecrans National Cemetery, San Diego, California.

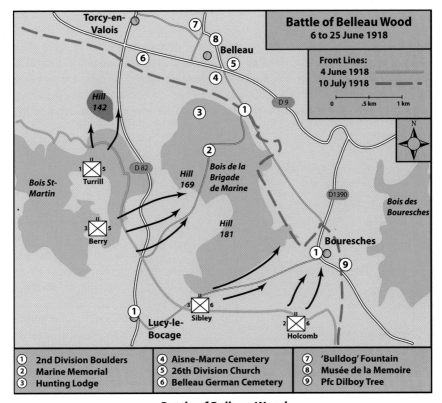

Battle of Belleau Wood

Support companies arrived and began digging defensive trenches.

A German infiltration attack led to confused hand-to-hand fighting among the heavy shrubs. Gunnery Sergeant Charles Hoffman, attempting to consolidate a position on the north slope of the hill, saw twelve enemy troops armed with five light machine guns crawling toward his group. Giving the alarm, he rushed the hostile detachment, bayoneted the two leaders, and forced the others to abandon their weapons and flee.[11]

Twelve hours later, three battalions entered the fields standing practically shoulder-to-shoulder as if on a parade ground to frontally assault Belleau Wood from the south and west. Back-lit by the setting sun, progress through the open fields before the forest became a deadly experience. Major Benjamin Berry's 3rd Battalion was cut down attempting to cross 400 meters of open ground – the attack over almost before it began. His surviving men hit the deck and remained so until able to withdraw after dark. Major Benton Sibley's 3rd Battalion, 6th Marine Regiment fared better, being

11 Gunnery Sergeant Charles F Hoffman of Brooklyn, New York, whose real name was Ernest August Janson, was awarded both the Army and Navy Medals of Honor (a simultaneous award that is no longer permitted). Sergeant Major Janson later served as the Marine Corps pallbearer for the burial of the Unknown Soldier on Armistice Day, 1921. Janson died in 1930 at age 51 after a brief illness. He is buried in Arlington National Cemetery. The reason for his adoption of the name Hoffman during his war service is unknown.

able to enter the woods to find a nest of machine guns and riflemen. The terrain broke the precise formations, but small groups continued the attack. The two right flank companies were cut to pieces by German guns, mortars and artillery. One platoon penetrated the enemy line, continued forward, and emerged into a wheat field near Bouresches. Major Thomas Holcolm's 2nd Battalion began an advance across 800 meters of wheat field without a leading artillery barrage and took enemy mahine-gun fire from the wood to the northwest and Bouresches to the northeast. Despite heavy casualties, the Marines captured the town in hand-to-hand fighting. By nightfall, only Sibley's battalion had gained a toe-hold in the wood. The Marine Corps suffered 1,087 casualties on that 6 June, more than in its prior 143 year history — combined.

Members of Medical Corps removing the wounded from Vaux, France, 22 July 1918. NARA

The battle became deadlocked with attack answered by counterattack as the battle became a contest of wills. Gradually, the wooded hilltop assumed a psychological importance out of proportion to its military value. The next day, with Marine positions under heavy German bombardment, diminutive 44-year-old First Gunnery Sergeant Daniel Daly visited all the positions of his 73rd Machine Gun Company rallying his men. At one point, while leading a local counterattack, Daly urged his men forward, famously shouting 'For Christ's sake men – come on! Do you want to live forever?'

On 10 June, the 6th Marine Regiment renewed the attack after an all-day artillery bombardment. Fighting in the dense forest was extremely difficult. Units easily became disoriented, the enemy had well-established positions, and American commanders did not know how to dislodge them. The contours of the ravines provided defensive positions that had to be taken by force of arms. At one point, a German machine gun section advanced close to Sergeant Daly's company and pinned it down. Daly, armed with only a .45-caliber automatic pistol and hand grenades, single-handedly charged and eliminated the enemy. Later that same day and under heavy fire, he brought in several wounded Marines during a German attack near the village of Bouresches. [12]

12　Sergeant Daniel Joseph Daly, from Glen Cove, New York, had already been awarded two Medals of Honor for his heroism in fighting during the Boxer Rebellion in China and against rebels in Haiti. For his actions in Belleau Wood, Daly received the Distinguished Service Cross, Navy Cross, and French *Croix de Guerre*. Daly survived the war to die in 1937 at age 63. He is buried in Cypress Hills National Cemetery, New York City.

By 14 June, the 4th Brigade had suffered fifty percent casualties and could not even determine how much of the wood it controlled. The exhausted men were given a seven day reprieve, being replaced by the 7th Regiment, which was unable to advance. The Marines returned to Bois de Belleau and, after another artillery bombardment, they captured the wood on 25 June. The next morning, headquarters received a terse report, '[Belleau] Woods now US Marine Corps entirely.'

Though militarily unimportant, the American victory was significant to both sides. The French took heart that they had a new ally capable of fighting the hated Hun. The Germans had five of their divisions, including the vaunted 5th Prussian Guards, mauled by the Americans. Ludendorff and his subordinates considered the combat capability of American troops as a war-losing event.

Battlefield Tour

The battlefield is best approached from the south through Lucy-le-Bocage, where a 2nd Division Memorial Boulder dated 1 June 1918 sits behind the church.[13] (49.05702, 3.27974)

> From Lucy-le-Bocage, proceed north 750 m to the access road on the right into the woods and continue 1.5 km to the memorial. (49.073146, 3.290791)

The fields north of Lucy were the site of the 5th Marine Regiment's attack of 6 June. The huge boulders, large trees, and thick undergrowth of Belleau Wood provide vivid images of the difficulty of this assault. The access road eventually leads to the open space of the **Marine Memorial**. Under a canopy of trees and in the center of the roadway, a black granite monolith displays a bas-relief of a shirtless marine attacking with rifle and bayonet. The plaque includes a brief description of the battle. The inscription also declares that the wood be known forevermore as Bois de la Brigade de Marine. Captured ordinance around the periphery of the clearing are aligned upon the memorial as if aiming upon a target. Dirt paths wind through the surrounding woods and remnants of shells or strongpoints are occasionally visible. Six bronze, ground-level plaques along a well-worn path to the left commemorate certain actions and present detailed descriptions of the battle, a map of the entire conflict, and recipients of the Medal of Honor.[14] The road continues to the border fence of the Aisne-Marne American Cemetery (see below), which is below the ridge on the north side of the wood. Passage directly into the cemetery is not possible, but the last German defensive trench that was captured on 25 June is near the fence.

The upper levels of the stone hunting lodge to the left (inside the cemetery fence) provided a German battalion headquarters dominating views until being overrun by the 43rd Marine Company in fierce fighting. (49.076866, 3.290793)

---

13 The path of the 2nd Division across the war's battlefields is identified by twenty-four such characteristic boulder monuments. Many will appear in this book's tour routes. A complete list may be found at: http://stenay-14-18.com/

14 Marine Gunnery Sergeant Ernest August Janson, Naval Reservist Lieutenant Orlando Henderson Petty, Lieutenant (jg) Weedon Edward Osbourne (posthumously), and Marine Gunnery Sergeant Fred William Stockham (posthumously).

Pass the Marine Memorial and follow the road down the hill to the cemetery entrance in Belleau. (49.081669, 3.292597)

Aisne-Marne American Cemetery
Rue des Chevaliers de Colomb, 02400 Belleau, France
Tel: +33 (0)3 23 70 70 90
See introduction for hours and website.

A massive gateway provides entry to the Aisne-Marne American Cemetery, followed by a lane that passes the offices and visitor's center to the grave plots where 2,288 men who died in regional fighting are buried under perfectly aligned rows of Latin Crosses and Stars of David. At the southern end and 80 feet up the ridge, a **French Romanesque Chapel** sits upon the frontline trenches dug by the 2nd Division after the battle. Engravings depict scenes of battle and insignia of the various units engaged in the area. The hole to the right of the entrance was made by a German tank shell in 1940 and has been purposely left unrepaired. The walls of the interior of the chapel are inscribed with the names of 1,060 troops who disappeared in the area and have no known grave.

A path leaves the left side of the Chapel and proceeds up the hill to the boundary fence previously mentioned. The ground still bears the imprints of American artillery shells and German rifle pits. A **2nd Division Memorial** rock rests to the left of the path along the service road behind the chapel with its bronze star dated 26 June 1918 marking the furthest advance of the Marine Brigade. The stone hunting lodge is further into the woods and to the east behind the chapel's spire. A memorial plaque above the doorway is dedicated to the 2nd Division.

A **Demarcation Stone** or **Vauthier marker**, placed by the Touring Club of France after the war to identify the front line on 18 July 1918 at the beginning of the Final Offensive, stands across the roadway intersection from the cemetery entrance. [15] (49.081714, 3.293272)

The **26th Division Memorial Church** stands directly across from the cemetery entrance. The village church was destroyed in later fighting and after the war this chapel was rebuilt by funds raised by the division's veteran organization. If it is not open, ask for the superintendent of the American cemetery to provide admission. Inside the church numerous plaques commemorate American units and individuals. The names of 2,700 men of the 26th Division killed in the war are inscribed on the walls. The stained-glass windows are particularly striking; two portray an American Doughboy and a French Poilu. Other windows include Frenchman who greatly influenced American history such as explorers Father Jacques Marquette and Samuel de Champlain, and French aristocrat and hero of the American Revolution Gilbert du Motier better known as the Marquis de Lafayette. (49.081714, 3.293272)

Proceed west 700 m on highway D9 from the entrance to the American Cemetery to the German Cemetery on the left. (49.083226, 3.283615)

---

15   The stones were sponsored by people from several different nationalities and designed by sculptor Paul Moreau Vauthier, a French veteran of the Verdun battles.

Battle of Belleau Wood

Demarcation Stone in Belleau, (right).

Marine Memorial in the Bois de la Brigade de Marine surrounded by field guns, (below).

The Aisne-Marne American Cemetery chapel.

West of Belleau toward Torcy (D9), the **German Military Cemetery** resounds with chiming from the carillon in the American Cemetery. In an almost treeless open field, 8,630 German dead are buried. Over 4,300 soldiers, most of them unidentified, rest in two mass graves. (49.083151, 3.283605)

Return to the American Cemetery entrance and turn north toward Givry (D1390). Proceed 500m into place du Général Pershing. (49.085444, 3.290721)

To the west are the château's stables – all that remain of the château that once dominated village life in prewar Belleau. The famous **'Bulldog' fountain**, so named because German troops claimed that the Marines fought like 'devil dogs,' is within its locked gates – the cemetery superintendent may provide access to the courtyard. Sources of water were always scarce on a battlefield, and this fountain provided succor to thirsty troops. The Marine Corps symbol of a bulldog was added after the war and the fountain carries a legend of providing increased longevity to any Marine who drinks from its waters – and all who come here do. (49.085455, 3.290464)

Musée de la Mémoire de Belleau 1914-1918
1 Place du Général Pershing, 02400 Belleau, France
Tel: +33 (0)3 23 82 03 63
Email: belleauwood@lesportesdelachampagne.com
Web: https://www.american-remembrance.com/
Open Friday and Saturday from 10:00 to 12:30 and 14:00 to 17:30; Sunday and Monday from 14:00 to 17:30; closed other days. (49.085257, 3.291029)
The museum holds a permanent exhibition on the American cemetery and the Marine Corps. A second space offers temporary exhibitions with themes related to the First World War.

Leave Belleau southeast from the 26th Division Memorial Church toward Bouresches (unnamed road) to the **2nd Division boulder** 550 m ahead on the right. (49.07732, 3.29688) The monument identifies the unit's furthest advance during the battle for Belleau Wood.
A second boulder is alongside the road in Bouresches commemorates the liberation of Bouresches on 6 June 1918. (49.065869, 3.309283)
From the second boulder, turn left, right, and left again (the unpaved road may require a short walk) to the tree memorial on the left side of the road. (49.06586, 3.31265)

The Greek oak tree, planted in 2010 within a protective metal enclosure, commemorates PFC George Dilboy of the 26th Division. Dilboy was defending the Bouresches train station on 18 July 1918 when fired upon by an enemy machine gun 100 meters distant. He opened fire at once from a standing position on the railroad track, fully exposed to view. Failing to silence the gun, he rushed forward through a wheat field with fixed bayonet toward the gun emplacement. Dilboy fell 25 yards short of the gun with his right leg nearly severed above the knee and with several other wounds. He continued to fire into the emplacement from a prone position, killing two of the enemy and forcing the gun crew to flee. Dilboy became the first Greek-American to be awarded the Medal of Honor.[16] (49.06586 3.31265)

From Bouresches, follow the Route de Bouresches to the Paris to Château-Thierry Road (D1003) and enter Vaux where a **2nd Division boulder** marks the advance of the division during the assault of 6 June. (49.04636, 3.35252)
Another 2nd Division boulder rests at an intersection with a minor road 2.8 km to the west marking the division's right flank on 1 June. (49.039781, 3.315434)
From Vaux, proceed east to Route du Monument and follow to its end. (49.041987, 3.371055)

The **American Aisne-Marne Memorial** stands upon a promontory (Hill 204) east of the American Cemetery. The American 3rd Division halted the German advance at Hill 204 on 7 June 1918. The 26th and 3rd Divisions finally reconquered the hill on 21 July 1918 during the Second Battle of the Marne.

American Aisne-Marne Memorial

The huge double colonnade commemorates the sacrifices of French and American soldiers who fought in this sector. The larger-than-life figures represent French-American friendship. A terrace on the side opposite the parking area offers dominating views of the Marne valley. A map emblazoned on its face shows the American advance during the Second Battle of the Marne.

Defense of the Marne
14 to 20 July 1918

Operation MARNE-REIMS, Ludendorff's fifth and last attempt to decide the war in Germany's favor, sought to expand the salient to the southwest, which would encircle Reims and appear to threaten Paris. East of Château-Thierry, the hills that ran along the south bank of the Marne River presented a natural defensive barrier with key crossing points in Château-Thierry and 10 kilometers east around the village of Mezy. The key battleground became the Surmelin Valley, following a small stream which flowed northward to join the Marne after cutting through the hills that would allow a deep penetration into the Allies' rear areas.

---

16   Private George Dilboy of Keane, New Hampshire was born in Izmir, Turkey. As a teenager he fought for Greek independence in two Balkan wars against Turkey and Bulgaria. Upon his return to America, he fought in the Mexican expedition against Pancho Villa in 1916. Dilboy was originally buried in the Aisne-Marne Cemetery, but family members requested he be re-interred in his Greek hometown. The grave was desecrated during the Greco-Turkish War of 1919-1920. President Warren Harding dispatched a naval vessel to retrieve the remains for burial in Arlington National Cemetery. He was 22 years old.

The 3rd Division's infantry units arrived on the scene on 3 June and took up defensive positions along the south bank of the Marne from Château-Thierry east to Varennes. The forests north of Jaulgonne, Chartèves, and Mont St-Pere offered the Germans concealed approaches to the Marne. The 30th and 38th Regiments prepared rifle pits along the river bank with a stronger defensive line along the railroad track 500 meters to the south. On his own initiative, the 38th Regiment commander, Colonel Ulysses Grant McAlexander, established defensive works atop Moulin Ridge at the eastern boundary of his sector.

American soldiers cross a pontoon bridge over the Marne River in Château-Thierry. (NARA)

OBJECTIVE	To force the Allies to pull French reserves out of Flanders by a feign attack upon Paris
FORCES	
AMERICAN:	3rd Division (Major General Joseph Dickman)
GERMAN:	Seventh Army (Generaloberst Max von Boehn)
RESULT	The Americans prevented the enemy from advancing past the Marne River defensive line
CASUALTIES	
AMERICAN:	12,000 total casualties
GERMAN:	Extensive
LOCATION	Château-Thierry is 90 km northeast of Paris; Mézy-Moulins is 10 km east of Château-Thierry

Battle

German artillery commenced bombardment of the division's line shortly after midnight on 15 July. Doughboys sheltered in dugouts and slit trenches as the fire intensified. The artillery lifted to a rolling barrage at 04:00 with two German divisions following. American riflemen lining the river banks shot boatloads of German soldiers attempting to cross the river. Six German attacks succeeded in driving a wedge 4,000 meters deep up the Surmelin Valley. Troops defending Ru Chailly Farm fought to the last man before being overwhelmed. The 30th 'Old Hickory' Division on the

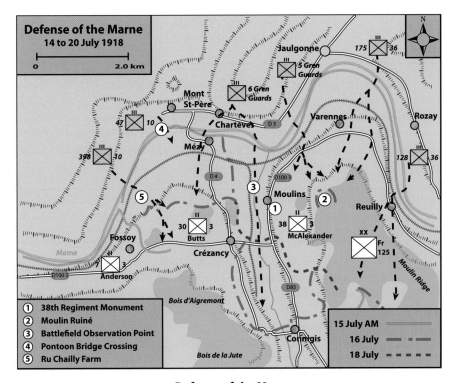

Defense of the Marne

3rd Division's left and the French 125th Division on its right withdrew under heavy pressure. With the situation desperate and outflanked to the east and west, Colonel Ulysses G McAlexander's 1st and 2nd Battalions, 38th Infantry stood and fought in previously prepared trenches on Moulin Ridge. The Moulin Ruiné was established as a final redoubt while he 3rd Battalion was pushed into the Bois d'Aigremont. Despite facing the enemy on three sides, McAlexander ordered his two separated commands toward the river, squeezing the German spearhead and exposing it to heavy shelling by 3rd Division artillery. The 28th Division reoccupied the river line east of Jaulgonne. By 17 July the German offensive had been stopped and Ludendorff ordered a withdrawal from the salient. The fighting had been so intense that the 38th Regiment lost 20 percent of its men; however, German losses among some units approached 60 percent. For example, the 6th Grenadiers located only 150 survivors out of an original compliment of 1,700 men. The 3rd Division's stubborn defense earned it the nickname 'Rock of the Marne,' which the unit proudly retains.

Battlefield Tour
The tour begins in the center of Château-Thierry along the north bank of the Marne west of the rue Carnot Bridge and passes to the east around Mézy-Moulins where the 3rd Division staged its defense of the river line.

From the rue Carnot Bridge in the center of Château-Thierry, move 350 m west along the north bank on avenue Jules Lefebvre to the memorial park. (49.043945, 3.398159)

The **3rd Division** erected a decidedly unattractive monument in the Place du Jean Moulin. Two six-foot-high stone walls are centered upon a high stone bearing a sword and dedicated to the division's heroic deeds in both world wars.

Across the street, an upright polished granite memorial inscribed with a 'V' is dedicated to Jean Moulin, a leader of the Parisian Resistance Movement, who was captured and tortured to death by the Nazis in 1943.

Continue 11 km east of Château-Thierry along highway D1003 and pass over Surmelin Creek just before entering Moulins. Stop at the stone in front of the Mairie. (49.059700, 3.520965)

In Moulins, a 2½-foot-high granite marker with a brass plaque on top erected by the **3rd Battle Group, 38th Regiment** stands in front of the Mairie in memory of the gallant heroes who fought and died here defending the Marne from 14 to 16 July 1918. The 38th Regiment held the 'Moulin Ruiné' position on the wooded ridge to the east against repeated German attack.

A 7-kilometer, self-guided trail has been established that starts at the monument and accesses the Moulin Ruiné and other locations on that sector of the battlefield. Look for a pamphlet *Promenade du Moulin Ruiné et du Bois Brûlé, 3e D.I. U.S., juillet 1918*. The guide is in French only. (Moulin Ruiné: 49.061603, 3.535293)

Proceed west along rue de Fossoy and stop near the railway spur crossing. (49.060378, 3.514973)

Captain Jesse Wooldridge's Company G, 38th Regiment defended Mézy in the wheat fields to the north with his 4th Platoon along this spur rail line. The company came under machine-gun fire from the 6th Grenadier Guards Regiment which successfully crossed against the 30th Regiment to the west. Captain Wooldridge personally led his 2nd Platoon in counterattack down the riverside rail embankment on his company's right flank. The action stopped the enemy advance, but all except Wooldridge and a private were killed. After a day of attack, counterattack, artillery shelling, and bayonet charge, the few surviving grenadiers were forced back to the river's edge to await transport to safety. [17]

McAlexander's Companies H and E were positioned to the east along the river bank with each company having two platoons forward and the other two in echelon. They presented intense rifle and machine-gun fire against German attempts to cross the river. Five platoons holding the line of thick brush at the river's edge were overrun in the predawn darkness, but the German advance was worn down by McAexander's

---

17 Major Jesse W Wooldridge died in 1963 at age 83. He is buried in Golden Gate National Cemetery, San Bruno, California.

defense in depth. Machine gunners, such as those led by Corporal John Connors, killed twenty boatloads of grenadiers. Connors continued to toss handgrenades into approaching boats until shot while holding a live grenade. Eventually all the defenders were killed or wounded. [18]

> Cross to the north bank of the river into Mont-St-Pére. Turn onto rue St-Nicolas and proceed to the river bank. (49.073123, 3.490096)

The south end of unpaved rue St-Nicolas provides a viewpoint of the river where the Germans constructed a pontoon bridge. The wheat fields where German grenadiers were exposed to American fire are plainly visible behind the thin brush line.

Second Battle of the Marne
17 July to 6 August 1918

In other sectors of the battlefield, the Allies became aware of the enemy's plans, and artillery bombarded German preparatory lines killing many of the tightly assembled troops. In contrast, German artillery shells fell upon essentially empty French and American lines as the Allies exercised the 'elastic defense,' with the main line outside the range of enemy cannon. Although the Germans were still able to fight their way across the river, the losses sustained were substantial and they were unable to advance. His infantry exhausted, Ludendorff called off the entire Operation MARNE-REIMS.

OBJECTIVE	To reduce the German salient which developed during the *Kaiserschlacht*
FORCES	
ALLIES:	Forty-four French divisions, eight American divisions, four British divisions, and two Italian divisions of the French Sixth Army (général Jean Degoutte), French Ninth Army (général Antoine de Mitry), and French Tenth Army (général Charles Mangin)
GERMAN:	Fifty-two Divisions of the First Army (Bruno von Mudra), Seventh Army (Generaloberst Max von Boehn), and Ninth Army (General Johannes von Eben)
RESULT	The last German offensive of the war failed under a French and American counterattack
CASUALTIES	
ALLIES:	132,700 total casualties including 12,000 Americans
GERMAN:	139,000 dead or wounded, 29,367 taken prisoner
LOCATION	Château-Thierry is 90 km northeast of Paris; Dormans is 25 km east of Château-Thierry and 14 km east of Moulins

---

[18]   Corporal John Joseph Connors of Pawtucket, Rhode Island, received the Distinguished Service Cross posthumously. Connors is buried in his home town; he was 22 years old.

Battle

On 18 July, the French Sixth and Tenth Armies, strengthened by the addition of five oversized American divisions,[19] attacked the throat of the salient that Ludendorff had created. The combined forces drove eastward with the US 1st Division seizing the heights of Buzancy overlooking the Soissons to Château-Thierry highway after a week of fierce combat. To its south, the 2nd Division in conjunction with the 1st Moroccan Colonial Regiment fought through the Forêt de Retz and also cut the critical highway. With the threat to cut off all German troops south of the Aisne River, the Germans executed a masterful fighting withdrawal back to the Vesle River. The two American

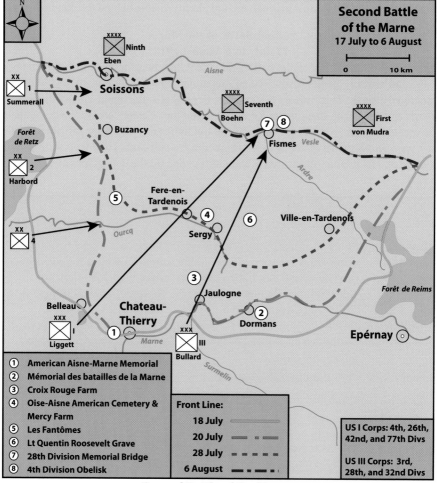

Second Battle of the Marne

_____

19 American divisions fielded two infantry brigades of two regiments each, a field artillery brigade with three regiments, a regiment of combat engineers, three machine gun battalions, plus signal, medical, and other supporting troops totaling 28,000 men — twice the size of Allied or German divisions.

divisions suffered 11,200 casualties. Fearlessly led by their officers, the officer death toll was inordinately high. In one instance, a battalion was being successfully led by a sergeant.

Further south, the 28th 'Keystone' Division from Pennsylvania teamed up with the 32nd 'Gemutlichkeit' Division from Michigan and Wisconsin to drive up the Château-Thierry- to Fismes Road. The 32nd led the way to Fismes where, on 7 August, it gratefully turned the front over to the 28th Division. The keystone men prowled the streets of Fismes going from house to house, searching out and clearing the town of the enemy.

The reduction of the Aisne-Marne salient had been an expensive learning process for the raw American troops – of the 300,000 men who participated, 50,000 were casualties. However, the tide of battle had swung to the Allies' favor, never to be reversed.

Aftermath

On 8 August, the British Army attacked across the front east of Amiens. Spearheaded by Australian and Canadian units and supported by 456 tanks, they advanced 13 km on the first day, once again crossing the Somme battlefields of summer 1916 and March 1918 while capturing 16,000 prisoners. The German lines were still well within French borders, but the German High Command realized that the war could not be won. Ludendorff described 8 August as the 'black day for the German Army.' Successive attacks to the north and south drove the Germans back to their last strong defensive positions in France – the Hindenburg Line.

Shell battered Fismette street with a German barricade. (NARA)

Battlefield Tour

The battlefield begins with a visit to a museum dedicated to the First and Second Battles of the Marne. Unfortunately, the museum is located some distance from the actual events. The tour returns to east of Château-Thierry near the Marne river defenses and follows the advance where American divisions, fighting under French Army commands, drove the enemy northward during increasingly difficult fighting.

> Leave Château-Thierry for Meaux 45 km to the west approaching the city from the north. Stop at the museum complex near the intersection of highways D 405 and D2405a (Route de Varreddes). (48.971432, 2.904724)

Musée de la Grande Guerre du Pays de Meaux
Rue Lazare Ponticelli, 77100 Meaux
Tel: +33 (0)1 60 32 14 18
Web: https://www.museedelagrandeguerre.eu/en.html
          Open daily except Tuesday from 09:30 to 18:00, Closed 1 May, 25 December, 1 January and early January. Admission fee
          Originally based upon a private collection, the newly constructed museum is now the largest in Europe dealing with the First World War. The diverse collection tackles the technical and military events with full uniforms from most of the warring countries, weaponry, and heavy equipment. Replica trenches and underground dugouts supplemented by objects from daily life on the front line illustrate the huge social changes and upheaval the war caused.

          The museum grounds hold the relocated **American Friends of France Monument** erected in 1932 by Americans to commemorate the French victory in the First Battle of the Marne in September 1914. The inscription reads:

> Here speak again the silent voices of heroic sons of France who dared all and gave all in the day of deadly peril turned back the flood of imminent disaster and thrilled the world by their supreme devotion.

          The 71-foot-tall statue of a naked woman standing proudly against the struggling and fallen bodies about her feet is sometimes called 'Hopeless Victory.' It remains the largest freestanding statue in France and marks the farthest German advance of the war.

American Friends of France Monument

> Dormans is 24 km east of Château-Thierry; follow signs to 'Memorial 1914 – 1918.' (49.071468, 3.646495)

Memorial to the Battles of the Marne (Mémorial des batailles de la Marne 1914-1918)
Parc du Château Avenue des Victoires, 51700 Dormans
Tel: +33 (0)3 26 59 14 18
Web: http://en.memorialdormans14-18.com/
          Open daily from 14:00 to 18:00 in April, May, September and October and from 10:30 to 18:30 in June, July and August.

The imposing and evocative Gothic and Romanesque structure was constructed on the grounds of a chateau in memory of the soldiers who fell during the Great War, particularly those who died on the banks of the Marne during the German offensives of 1914 and 1918.

The interior stone block walls are inscribed with individual military unit names. A crypt with altar and kneelers provides a place of reverence. Fifty-two steps lead to the esplanade and the Lanterne des Morts (tall tower holding a beacon to the dead). From the chapel, 105 steps lead to a circular walkway offering spectacular views over the Marne Valley and surrounding vineyards in every direction for some distance. To the east a covered walkway leads to an ossuary stacked with coffins of 1500 French unknowns and two urns containing the ashes of a deportee from Dachau and earth from the French cemeteries in Italy. Tablets on the walls of the covered walkway present Joffre and Foch, the two marshals who won the Battles of the Marne, and list the armies, corps and divisions that participated.

> The Croix Rouge farm memorial is along highway D3 18 km north of Dormans. (49.13271, 3.52122)

On 24 July, the 42nd Division moved to Château-Thierry to relieve the embattled 26th Division. On a windy and cold 26 July, its 167th (Alabama) Regiment, with its sister regiment the 168th (Iowa), attacked across a one-mile-square open field against a fortified, walled compound known as Croix Rouge Farm. German defenses included twenty-five 7.92-mm water-cooled machine guns sited to provide interlocking fire. The 1st Battalion assault started in late afternoon but failed, and the battalion was pinned down for about an hour in the open field. A renewed assault two hours later by four platoons totaling 110 men was successful, despite suffering 60 percent casualties. The 3rd Battalion suffered similar levels of casualties, attacking from the south and southwest before fending off the last German counterattack with fixed bayonets. By the end of the day's fighting, 162 were dead and over 1,100 wounded. German dead totaled 283.

A three-meter-high bronze statue represents Sergeant William Johnson Frazer of Greenville, Alabama being carried from the battlefield on 26 July. Frazer, a member of Company D Assault Force, was hit twice by German machine-gun fire. He lay on the no man's land for 17 hours before being picked out of a shell hole and evacuated. The memorial was erected

Croix Rouge Farm. NARA

by Frazer's son and commemorates the 42nd Division's bloody battle at Croix Rouge farm.

> Proceed 10 km north of Croix Rouge Farm on highway D2 to the Oise-Aisne American Cemetery. (49.200941, 3.549050)

The Alabama and Iowa Regiments followed the retreating enemy for 10 kilometers to the south bank of the Ourcq River where they were joined by the full Rainbow Division. It attacked across the river on 28 July. The 167th (New York) and 166th (Ohio) Regiments fought at Meurcy Farm just south of the present Oise-Aisne American Cemetery. After four days of hard fighting by both sides, a massive German retreat began on 2 August 1918. The 42nd Division's casualties totaled 5,653.

Famed American poet Joyce Kilmer enlisted in the 7th Regiment, New York National Guard in April 1917, a few days after the United States entered the First World War. Sergeant Kilmer eventually sought more hazardous duty and was transferred to the military intelligence section of his regiment and assigned to lead scouting patrols in no man's land. On 30 July, Kilmer volunteered to accompany Major 'Wild Bill' Donovan when Donovan's 1st Battalion 165th Regiment was sent to lead the attack. During the course of the day, Kilmer led a scouting party to find the position of a German machine gun. Sometime later his comrades found him peering over the edge of a knoll. Kilmer was dead – shot in the head.[20]

Oise-Aisne American Cemetery
Chemin départemental 2, 02130 Seringes-et-Nesles, France
Tel: +33(0)3 23 82 21 81
See introduction for hours and web address.

The Oise-Aisne American Cemetery was created on the very spot where the 42nd Division fought and many of its 6,012 graves hold men from that unit. A curving colonnade stands at the far end of a gentle slope from the entrance. The colonnade is flanked on one side by a map room providing locations of area engagements and on the other side by a chapel. Both are beautifully constructed of rose-colored sandstone inscribed with implements of war. The Wall of the Missing bears 241 additional names.

> A somber memorial to the Second Battle of the Marne stands 14 km west of Seringes-et-Nesles beside highway D229. (49.214839, 3.411472)

Les Fantômes
02210 Oulchy-le-Château, France

Les Fantômes, a sculpture on the Butte Chalmont near Oulchy-le-Château, overlooks the plain where thousands of Allied soldiers launched their attacks on the northern banks of the Ourcq River and provides panoramic views of the Ourcq to the south and Fère-en-Tardenois to the east where the outcome of the Second Battle of

---

20   Sergeant Joyce Kilmer, author of the poem 'Trees', was 31 years of age. He is buried in the Oise-Aisne American Cemetery in Plot B Row 9 Grave 15.

Second Battle of the Marne

Peristyle Altar at the rear of the Oise-Aisne American Cemetery. The inscription reads, 'In Sacred Sleep They Rest.'

The memorial fountain in Chamery commemorates Lieutenant Quentin Roosevelt .

Les Fantômes at the Butte de Chalmont.

the Marne was decided. At the entrance a statue of a woman wearing a round shield symbolizes France in victory and hope. The approach up a long grass slope is lined by two memorial walls; on the left is the complete order of battle — the generals and the units involved in the Second Battle of the Marne. The right wall describes the conquest of the Butte de Chalmont on 25 and 26 July 1918.

Eight, 25-foot-tall granite figures, each representing 170,000 French soldiers killed during the war, stand huddled, arms hanging limp, heads hang listlessly, eyes blank. Seven of the figures represent a young recruit, a sapper, a machine-gunner, a grenadier, a colonial soldier, an infantryman, and an aviator. The accoutrements of warfare are beside them; a Lebel rifle rests against one, another cradles a machine gun, a third carries two sacks of grenades, another rests his fingertips on a pick handle. The seven are in uniform while they surround, as if to protect, the just fallen eighth figure – naked, struggling with his shroud. They are the dead – Les Fantômes – the phantoms of war. A more griping, haunting remembrance would be difficult to find. This outstanding work was accomplished by sculptor Paul Landowski. [21]

Chamery is 5.3 km east of the Oise-Aisne American Cemetery alongside highway D14. Stop at the roadside fountain. (49.193367, 3.615973)

During the struggle for the Marne Valley, members of the 95th Aero Squadron engaged German planes in the skies above. On 14 July 1918, 1st Lieutenant Quentin Roosevelt, the youngest of former President Theodore Roosevelt's four sons, took to the air. The American was flying a second-rate Nieuport 28 aircraft when he was attacked by three superior Fokker Chasses. Roosevelt was shot twice in the head during the ensuing dogfight and his plane crashed behind enemy lines.

A fountain erected by the family remembering 1st Lieutenant Quentin Roosevelt stands in the little village of Chamery inscribed with the words of is father: 'Only those are fit to live who do not fear to die.' A white tombstone on the hillside above the town 750 meters to the southeast identifies Quentin Roosevelt's original grave site where German troops buried the dead airman with full military honors.[22] (49.19056 3.62417)

Fismes is 15 km north of Chamery. Proceed to the bridge that crosses the Vesle River and separates Fismes from Fismette. (49.312536, 3.679567)

After the German failure in the Second Marne assault, they began an

---

21   Born in Paris to a French mother and a Polish immigrant father, Landowski was 39 years old when his unit, the 132nd Régiment d'Infanterie, was mobilized on August 6, 1914 at the very start of the Great War. He spent four years at the front, was awarded a *Croix de Guerre* in 1917, and somehow managed to survive. He is best known for Christ the Redeemer, the enormous art deco statue of Jesus that stands above Rio de Janeiro.

22   On 22 September 1955, the remains of the pilot were transferred to the Normandy American Cemetery in Colleville-sur-Mer, France at the request of his family such that he could be buried alongside his brother, Brigadier General Theodore Roosevelt Jr, who died during the Second World War in Normandy. Quentin was 21 years old, his brother was 56.

organized retreat on 20 July eventually establishing a defensive line along the banks of the Vesle River on 3 August.

The battles over Fismes and Fismette exhibited an extreme violence during street fighting that seldom occurred during the war. The 28th 'Keystone' Division, formed from the Pennsylvania National Guard and as part of général Degoutte's Fourth French Army, fought against stormtrooper attacks and flamethrowers for nearly a month while Fismes exchanged hands five times, resulting in the destruction of 90 percent of the town. Attempts to establish a bridgehead across the river in Fismette were met with artillery, gas, and attacks from the surrounding hillsides. Events culminated on the morning of 27 August when two companies of the 112th Regiment totaling 236 men experienced a determined German attack leaving only 30 survivors. As a consequence, Pershing would never again allow French generals to command American troops.

A memorial bridge built by the Commonwealth of Pennsylvania in homage to the **28th Division's** operations in Champagne crosses the Vesle River to connect the villages of Fismes and Fismette. The gateposts carry engravings of the unit's emblem, coats of arms of the United States and the State of Pennsylvania, and bas-reliefs of helmeted American soldier's faces. The posts are topped with statues of Ladies of Peace and Agriculture.

Other Sites of Interest:

An obelisk bearing the cloverleaf insignia of the **4th Division** stands north of the Vesle River alongside highway N31 only 2.4 km west of Fismes. The monument stands near a position which was called Le Château du Diable (The Devil's Castle – in the forest to the southeast). The 4th, 28th, and 77th Divisions fought numerous engagements in and around the chateau as German troops contested their beachhead over the Vesle River only 220 meters to the south. (49.310694, 3.647325)

A **1st Division Memorial**, 40 km west of Fismes (or 9 km south of Soissons), identifies where the division broke the German lines and assaulted the Buzancy Heights on 21 July 1918. In the ensuing engagement the division suffered 2,213 soldiers killed and 6,347 wounded. The fight was so intense that three quarters of the whole division's

An example of the US 4th Division's monuments stands outside Fismes.

The US 1st Division Memorial outside Buzancy presents the standard design for this unit's First World War Monuments.

infantry officers became casualties. Plaques attached to the monument and the ground below list the names of those killed and missing in action. (49.313938, 3.336753)

Ypres-Lys Offensive
19 August to 11 November 1918

The sector of Western Front extending from the English Channel south through Ypres was manned by Belgian, British, and French armies under King Albert of Belgium. In late August and early September, the British Second and Fifth Armies, assisted by the American II Corps composed of the 27th Division from the New York National Guard and 30th 'Old Hickory' Division named after Andrew Jackson, wiped out the Lys salient.

OBJECTIVE	To eliminate the German salient around Ypres.
FORCES	
AMERICAN:	27th and 30th Divisions, later the 37th and 91st Divisions as elements of the Army Group Flanders (King Albert of Belgium)
GERMAN:	Fourth Army (General der Infanterie Sixth von Armin)
RESULT	The Allied armies continued to push across Belgium until the Armistice
CASUALTIES	
AMERICAN:	27th and 30th Divisions: 2,100 casualties 37th and 91st Divisions: 2,600 casualties
GERMAN:	Uncertain
LOCATION	Ypres is 265 km north of Paris; Vierstraat is 7 km south of Ypres.

Battle

The 27th and 30th Divisions served with the British Army from their arrival in Europe in May 1918. The 30th Division entered the front line on 18 August and the 27th Division on 23 August. Their participation in the Ypres-Lys Offensive began on 31 August when both divisions moved slowly forward against determined German resistance. That afternoon the 27th Division reached the area where the Kemmel Monument stands. The 27th Division was relieved on 3 September and the 30th Division the next day. Both units moved south to the region near St. Quentin to join the Somme Offensive of 23 to 30 September.

In mid-October at the request of Supreme Commander of the Allied Armies, général Ferdinand Foch, Pershing dispatched the 37th 'Buckeye' Division from Ohio, and the 91st 'Wild West' Division from the Washington National Guard to the French Army of Belgium to give impetus to the drive to cross the Scheldt River as part of the Hundred Days Offensive (see next chapter). A general attack began in this area on 31 October and continued intermittently until hostilities ended on 11 November. On the first day of the assault, the 91st Division easily occupied its objective at a forest known as Spitaals Bosschen, but was then delayed as the French division on its right failed to keep up and exposed its right flank to severe hostile enfilade fire which continued throughout the day.

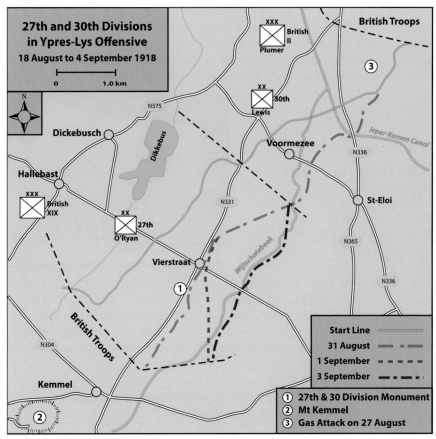

27th and 30th Divisions in Ypres-Lys Offensive
18 August to 4 September 1918

American Participation in the Ypres-Lys Offensive

On 1 November it became evident that the Germans were withdrawing and the 37th and 91st Divisions pushed forward rapidly. The 37th Division advanced about 15 kilometers to the Escaut River. The 91st advanced about the same distance to a position close to Audenarde which it occupied on 2 November.

Battlefield Tour

This side trip to the area where American forces fought while attached to the British Army traverses the battlefield of Ypres, where British and German Armies bled each other white during four massive encounters from 1914 to 1918. The area is rife with memorials, cemeteries, museums, and battlefield artifacts. This short tour describes only those locations related to American efforts, but time should be allowed to fully explore the Ypres battlefield.

The memorial is south of Vierstraat between Ypres and Kemmel on highway N331. (50.797833, 2.849033)

The **Kemmel American Monument** commemorates the service and sacrifices of the 27th and 30th Divisions who fought attached to the British Army from 18 August to 4 September 1918. This monument stands upon a low platform and consists of a rectangular white stone block with soldier's helmet upon a wreath carved on a low column before it. A terrace enclosed by a railing surrounds the monument.

> Proceed to the cemetery 3.5 km southeast of Waregem, Belgium. (50.873595, 3.452106)

Flanders Field American Cemetery and Memorial
Wortegemseweg 117
8790 Waregem, Belgium
Tel: +32 (0)5 660 11 22
See introduction for hours and website.

US 27th and 30th Divisions Monument at Vierstraat

The only First World War American cemetery in Belgium occupies a peaceful site where 368 of America's military dead remain and an additional 68 missing are commemorated. Many fell at Spitaals Bosschen in the closing days of the First World War. Paths lead to three of the corners of the cemetery where benches and commemorative urns occupy circular retreats.

> Oudenaarde is 12 km east of Waregem; the memorial is in the center of Oudenaarde near General Pershingstraat. (50.846633, 3.602366)

The **Audenarde American Monument** is in the town of Oudenaarde (Audenarde), Belgium. The golden-yellow limestone monument bears the shield of the United States flanked by two stone eagles and stands at the end of a small park. It commemorates the service and sacrifice of the 40,000 American troops of the 37th and 91st Divisions which, in October and November 1918, fought in the vicinity as units attached to the Army Group Flanders, commanded by Albert I, King of the Belgians. Both divisions participated in the offensive from near Waregem toward the Scheldt River, beginning on 31 October.

The Hundred Days Offensives

Although the *Kaiserschlacht* achieved considerable territorial gains, it secured no strategic objective. Ludendorff was left with few choices to even continue the war. The German High Command could not replace the loses incurred and the ever stronger American Army brought the manpower advantage to the Allied side.

By September 1918, the French Army was once again an offensive force after the dramatic consequences of its 1917 mutiny. Général Foch's plans for the fall of 1918 included coordinated actions by the allied armies against the entire front from Ypres to Verdun to prohibit Germany from moving troops from quiet sectors to face allied offensives – a feat that had served them well in the past.

Battle of the St-Quentin Canal
29 September to 2 October 1918

During the last week of September, the British Third Army attacked on either side of Cambrai to the north and the French First Army did the same on either side of St-Quentin to the south. Meanwhile in the center, British Fourth Army attacked the along a 19-kilometer front between Cambrai and St-Quentin.

The final line of resistance incorporated the natural barrier of the St-Quentin Canal, which connected the Somme and Scheldt Rivers. North of St-Quentin, the canal ran through a 5,670-meter-long (3.5-mile) tunnel opened in 1810 by Napoleon Bonaparte. Barges moored in the tunnel provided shelter, supplies, and hospitals for a German division. The ground above was honeycombed with galleries providing access to pillboxes, machine-gun nests, and escape openings. The steep banks of the canal were festooned with trenches and machine guns. The main defense line was west of the tunnel, where multiple lines of tangled barbed wire formed strongpoints known as 'the Knoll,' and at the Tombois, Quennemont, and Guillemont farms. The underground sections of the canal provided a key crossing point.

OBJECTIVE	To assault the St-Quentin Tunnel as part of a larger action to penetrate the Hindenburg Line
FORCES	
ALLIES:	US II Corps (Major General GW Read); British IX Corps (Lieutenant-General Walter P Braithwaite); Australian Corps (Lieutenant-General Sir John Monash)
GERMAN:	Two corps of the German Second Army (General der Infanterie Adolph von Carlowitz)
RESULT	The Hindenburg Line was broken, and allied troops pushed the German Second Army back to the German Beaurevoir Line.
CASUALTIES	
ALLIES:	5,801 American casualties; 2,577 Australian casualties; significantly fewer British casualties
GERMAN:	Estimated 5,969 taken prisoner
LOCATION	Cambrai is 175 km north of Paris; Bony is 25 km south of Canbrai.

Battle

A bombardment against enemy batteries from 1,634 guns started during the night of 26/27 September, with a heavy concentration of gas shells – including dreaded mustard gas. After a day of cold rain, assault units began the attack shrouded in the shell smoke and early morning mists of 29 September with the 27th and 30th Divisions and the British 46th (North Midland) Division in line from north to south. The men of British 137th Brigade scrambled down the sides of the 10-meter-wide canal and swam the canal using life jackets and whatever would float to cross the 2-to-3-meter-deep water barrier. They fought their way up the eastern bank effectively piercing the Hindenburg defenses between Bellicourt and Bellenglise.

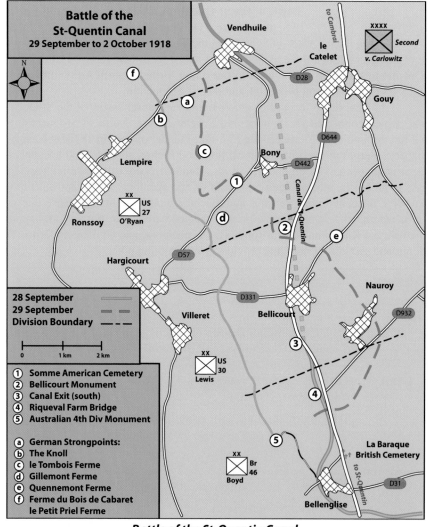

Battle of the St-Quentin Canal

The 30th Division overcame three lines of wire as well as three trench systems and seized Bellicourt at the southern entrance of the tunnel with the help of an intrepid Sergeant Joseph Adkison, Company C, 119th Regiment. With visibility limited by fog and smoke, German machine-gun fire pinned down Adkison's platoon. Alone, he rushed across the fifty meters of open ground directly into the face of the hostile machine gun, kicked the gun from the parapet into the enemy trench, and at the point of the bayonet captured the three men manning the gun. Later that same day, Sergeant Adkison was severely wounded by an exploding artillery shell, receiving wounds to his left arm, left hip and left leg. [23]

Although they broke the line and advanced as far as Nauroy, 30th Division was attacked from the rear by German troops exiting the tunnel galleries. The 5th Australian Division responded and eliminated the enemy.

Farther north, the American 27th Division was in trouble. Replacing a British division only a few days before the attack, they arrived to find the planned jumping-off trenches still occupied by the Germans. Minor assaults on 27 and 28 September had failed to dislodge stubborn German defenses and strongpoints such as the 'Knoll' remained in enemy hands. Because the advance was delayed by these German positions, they lost contact with the creeping barrage. Antitank fire quickly disabled allotted tanks. Pleas to the British artillery battalions to call back the barrage were refused. German machine guns pressured the American left flank where British troops to the north lagged behind. The units lost contact with each other in the dense fog and smoke and fell victim to confused fighting. Most officers quickly became casualties, but the troops advanced up the slope of the tunnel in small, isolated groups, some of which crossed the canal line as far as Bony. Reserve battalions were attacked from the rear, while bypassed strongpoints remained centers of resistance.

At noon the 3rd Australian Division was ordered to assault the many German positions bypassed by the American advance. Troops of the two countries mixed, with many of the 27th Division refusing to leave the field. The Australians passed through the American troops and continued the attack. By midnight the main German line of resistance withdrew to behind the canal. The division's 107th Regiment lost 335 killed and 884 wounded – the equivalent of a battalion of men, the most casualties suffered by an American unit on one day in the war.

On 30 September, the 27th Division was ordered into support, but the frontline troops continued to fight alongside the Australians. The remainder of the Hindenburg Line was cleared, and again Bony was entered but still not cleared until the following day. Ferme du Bois de Cabaret strongpoint was taken in a hand-grenade attack against desperate resistance. Constant pressure forced the defenders back to the Beaurevoir Line, 4 kilometers east of the canal.

At 01:30 on 1 October, the 27th Division was relieved and sent to the rear area. The men may have been lacking in coordination and leadership, but they were never short of courage. The battle was short but intense, as demonstrated by the United States awarding nine Medals of Honor.

---

23   Sergeant Joseph Adkison, from Shelby County, Tennessee was awarded the Medal of Honor. He died in 1965 at age 73 and in buried in his home state.

Battlefield Tour
The tours reviews sites along the underground section of the canal between Cambrai and St-Quentin.

> The village of Bony is 25 km south of Cambrai. Continue west of the village to the cemetery. (49.985564, 3.216026)

Somme American Cemetery
American Cemetery, 02420 Bony, France
Tel: +33 (0)3 23 66 87 20
See introduction for visitor information and website.

The cemetery is located on the site of strong German positions and thus a true battlefield cemetery. It contains 1,844 graves, including three Medal of Honor recipients, arranged in a perfectly symmetrical pattern. The corner posts of the cemetery wall are topped with beautifully carved military scenes and the small stone chapel displays an ornately carved bronze door. The chapel walls list the names of 333 soldiers whose remains were never located.

> The memorial is less than 1 km south of Bony alongside highway D1044. (49.975151, 3.233003)

The **Bellicourt American Monument** commemorates the sacrifices of 90,000 American troops who fought with the British Army during 1917 and 1918. From the east, a gated roadway approaches the broad stone stairway that ascends to the intricately carved face of a rectangular stone block. The western façade has a map of the actions of the 27th and 30th Divisions during their attack upon the Hindenburg Line as well as a table of orientation. Its position is directly on top of the underground canal and within the Hindenburg Line. The direction from which the Americans attacked can be viewed from the memorial's west terrace, which also overlooks the Vallée de Bony, where American troops sheltered from enemy guns while preparing for the assault. The Quennemont Ferme defenses were on the high ground appearing in the distance as a brush-bordered plot. The British and American starting positions were approximately along A26 Autoroute, two to three kilometers west of the canal. The German strongpoints are accessible only via farm roads and are of little interest.

> Continue south 1 km to the canal exit. (49.951289, 3.236088)

The southern canal exit also offers a small barge museum and tourist information office. A steep forest path leads down to the canal and its entrance, however, access to the still-working canal tunnel is strictly prohibited. A concrete pillbox, apparently used as a German command post, remains on the western shoulder above the canal entrance; it can be entered, but bring illumination. The northern exit of the canal near Macquincourt is more difficult to access and offers little of interest.

St-Quentin Canal

Somme American Cemetery, (right).

South exit of the Riqueval Tunnel, (right).

Bellicourt Monument honoring American soldiers who attacked and conquered the Hindenburg Line, (below).

Australian 4th Division Memorial, (right).

Other Sites of Interest:
A rural road leads from Riqueval to the famous **Riqueval Farm Bridge** captured by the 6th Battalion, North Staffordshire Regiment in a desperate race before it could be destroyed by the enemy. The structure remains almost exactly as it appeared in 1918. A plaque commemorates the event. Another ruined German pillbox is barely visible in the underbrush on the east end of the bridge. (49.939985, 3.242129)

Many small villages east of the Cambrai- to St-Quentin road contain small memorials to their liberation by American divisions. The **Memorial Obelisk to the 4th Australian Division** is west of Bellenglise; unfortunately, accessible only over a rough farm road. Despite its isolated location, the site has beautifully manicured trees, shrubs, and lawn, and the high location offers views across the Hindenburg Line battlefield. (49.930673, 3.226649)

The **La Baraque British Cemetery**, which holds 60 British burials from local fighting, is 800 meters northeast of Bellenglise immediately east of highway D1044. (49.927899, 3.249951) A memorial obelisk to the **British 46th Division** is accessed via a dirt track along highway D1044 300 meters south of the cemetery. (49.924801, 3.250719)

Champagne Offensive
26 September to 28 October 1918

Champagne had been the scene of dreadful combat between French and German forces for four years with massive casualties on both sides. Five great battles took place in the area: the winter battle of 1914/1915; a powerful French offensive on 25 September 1915; a French assault upon Moronvilliers in April and May 1917; defeat of the German offensive of 15 July 1918; and the victorious Franco-American Offensive of 26 September 1918. Thus, the elevated plains of Champagne's grain-growing region rank behind only Ypres, Verdun, and Somme in terms of the numbers of casualties; however, the Champagne battles have largely disappeared from view, unfortunately not even mentioned in some histories of the war.

In conjunction with the American Offensive in the Meuse-Argonne (see below), the French Fourth Army was to attack between Reims and the Argonne Forest. Although they made progress, advancing four kilometers in four days, they trailed behind the American advance in the Argonne, and the increasing separation concerned military planners. By 30 September, the French offensive was stalled by resistance south of Blanc Mont, a boomerang-shaped height that marked the last natural defensive feature south of the Aisne River. With customary German thoroughness, it had been strengthened by a network of trenches, shelters, and barbed-wire entanglements. At général Pétain's request, two American divisions were sent to assist in taking the hill.

OBJECTIVE	To eliminate German resistance west of the Forêt d'Argonne.
FORCES	
ALLIES:	Two American divisions and two French divisions of the French Fourth Army (général de division Henri Gouraud)
GERMAN:	Third Army's XII Saxon Corps (General der Kavallerie Hans Krug von Nidda)

RESULT	Germany abandoned the Champagne Region.
CASUALTIES	
AMERICAN:	7,386 killed and wounded
FRENCH:	Unknown
GERMAN:	Unknown killed and wounded; 2,296 taken prisoner
LOCATION	Reims is 140 km northeast of Paris; Sommepy-Tahure is 50 km east of Reims

Battle

On 2 October, the 2nd Division – of Belleau Wood fame – arrived and immediately cleared a section of the Essen Trench on the western end of their area of operation. The division's commander, Major General John Lejeune, had no intention of a frontal assault against the concrete pillboxes of Blanc Mont ridge. Instead he split the division to effect a pincer attack with the unit's 3rd Brigade on the right and 4th Brigade (Marines) on the left. At 05:50 on 3 October, the soldiers and Marines, accompanied by French tanks, left their trenches after a brief artillery preparation to follow behind a rolling barrage. The infantry brigade, however, first had to clear their frontline trenches of casualties after a brief German artillery preparation supporting a spoiling raid earlier that morning. Despite the initial setback, they were soon atop the ridge and moving along the arc of its summit. By 08:30, the eastern half of the ridge was in American hands and a defensive front was established as far east as Médéah Farm.

The Marine Brigade also moved forward, taking position after position in hand-to-hand fighting, and reaching the summit at approximately 08:30. The French failed to retain Essen Hook trench, however, and were unable to advance on the Marine left flank, leaving the western portion of the hill in enemy hands. The Americans were in a salient with enfilade artillery and machine-gun fire pouring on them while they sheltered in captured German trenches. While the infantry brigade continued its advance northward, the Marines dispatched forces to establish a left flank when enemy counterattacks fell upon their line. German troops trapped in the triangle between the two American brigades eventually surrendered.

During the night the Germans moved machine guns and artillery forward to bring enormous firepower against the American flanks. Germany's air superiority supported effective targeting by German batteries. At daybreak the 15th Bavarian Division launched two counterattacks from Médéah Farm and St-Étienne-à-Arnes, attempting a pincer of its own; both were beaten back with great losses. On 5 October, 3rd Battalion, 6th Marine Regiment stormed the last of the Blanc Mont strongpoints on the western end of the ridge, capturing 213 prisoners and 75 machine guns. The remainder of the day was spent consolidating their positions. With the French finally moving along the western slopes of the hill, the advance continued on 6 October. The Marines and French 22nd Division were stopped from entering St-Étienne-à-Arnes by intense fire. The ridge before the village shielded enemy troop movements and tunnels connected strongholds in the cemetery.

The 36th 'Lone Star' Division took over for the 2nd Division and, supported by two French tank battalions, took the village the next day. The advance continued against weakening German resistance while units made their escape over the Aisne River. The 21-kilometer pursuit was a vicious struggle against strongpoints manned by sacrificial rearguards. Allied pursuit across the river was defeated by strong German positions and by the lack of intact bridges. The American contribution to the offensive was terminated on 28 October, when the last German pocket south of the river was cleared of the enemy. The fearless capture of strategic Blanc Mont permitted the advance of the entire French Fourth Army in coordination with the American First Army in the Meuse-Argonne.

Battlefield Tour

The battlefield occupied 120 square kilometers of desolate waste resulting from trench warfare and along a front running from Reims to the Forêt d'Argonne. In 1918, the front ran along an east-west line near the

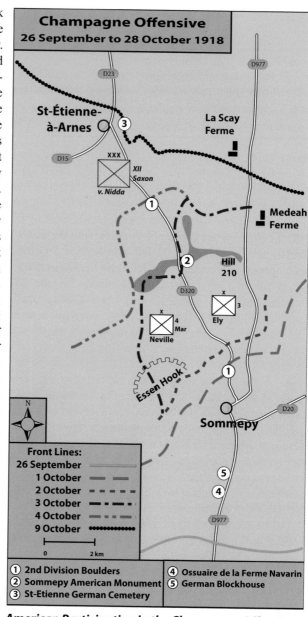

Champagne Offensive
26 September to 28 October 1918

Front Lines:
26 September
1 October
2 October
3 October
4 October
9 October

0   2 km

1 2nd Division Boulders
2 Sommepy American Monument
3 St-Etienne German Cemetery
4 Ossuaire de la Ferme Navarin
5 German Blockhouse

American Participation in the Champagne Offensive

Ferme de Navarin, midway between Sommepy and Souain. The 60-meter-high Navarin Ridge stretched 4 kilometers to the north from near Orfeuil in the east, through Médéah Ferme, to Blanc Mont in the west. The extremes of the battlefield are now bordered by military cemeteries, including twenty-six French necropolises and ossuaries to the south and numerous German cemeteries to the north. The Camp Militaire de Suippes remains a restricted area of destroyed villages and shell-laden fields. Despite the epic battles fought here during much of the First World War, remarkably few locations provide memorials. For Americans the exception is Blanc Mont.

The tour begins in Sommepy-Tahure, which was liberated by the French 62th Division, and continues north over fiercely defended ground. Sommepy-Tahure was originally named only Sommepy, which means 'the source of the Py,' a small stream that has its source in the village. Tahure was a village destroyed during the war whose ruins are now inaccessible in the military camp of Suippes. The village is remembered by having its name combined with Sommepy.

The German Army entered Sommepy on 2 September 1914 and occupied the town for four years. Reconstruction began in 1920, partially financed by funds raised in the United States.

The **15th century Église de Sommepy-Tahure** surmounts a hill in the center of the town. Only the west portal of the church survived the war and its façade still bears damage from bullets and shells. A broad stairway leads up to the church on its west side. A 2nd Division boulder, which identified the town as divisional headquarters, stands to the left of the base of the stairway. (49.250629, 4.555911)

The church grounds hold a memorial stone dedicated to the 5th and 6th Marine Regiments and the division commander General John Lejeune who fought to liberate the area north of Sommepy on 3 and 4 October (exact location uncertain).

The hillside behind the church along rue de l'Hôtel Dieu holds small stone remembrances to the *villages détruit*[24] of the region and a German concrete pillbox constructed in 1914 that forms the entrance to an underground dugout. (49.250911, 4.556637)

Leave Sommepy-Tahure to the north passing a 2nd Division boulder monument, one of four such markers on the Blanc Mont battlefield, beside the highway 1.4 km to the north. It identifies the right flank of the unit at the start of its assault upon Mont Blanc. (49.257731, 4.547721)

The fields to the left were crossed by the 4th Marine Brigade in its assault on the ridge. Even though the rolling hills that approach the monument from the south do not appear steep, their openness deprived attackers any opportunity for cover.

The summit of the crescent-shaped ridge holds the **Sommepy American Monument** erected by the American Battle Monuments Commission after the war to commemorate the 70,000 troops that fought locally as units of the Fourth French Army. Seventy-six stairs provide access to the rectangular golden-yellow limestone observation tower which affords excellent views of surrounding vestiges of World War I trenches, dugouts and gun emplacements. The tower is emblazoned with the American eagle and the parapet is decorated with bas-reliefs of military equipment. Trench lines and entrances into underground dugouts are still visible within the grounds

---

24 After the war, it was decided that the land previously occupied by villages destroyed the fighting that could not be rebuilt would be incorporated into other communes and to preserve their memory. They were declared *villages détruit,*

of the monument. The Americans fought a desperate struggle to control these positions against repeated German counterattacks. The interior is open weekdays from 09:00 to 17:00 and on weekends to 18:00; closed 25 December and 1 January. No admission charge. Exterior grounds open during daylight hours all year.

A white boulder monument erected to the **2nd Division** is visible to the north at the edge of the road. The site marks the forward advance achieved by the 5th Marine Regiment during the night of 4/5 October. (49.294900, 4.517941)

Continue into St-Étienne-à-Arnes and turn toward Semide (D41) to the nearby cemetery on the right. (49.314236, 4.499852)

The **St-Étienne-à-Arnes German Military Cemetery** holds 12,541 burials under metal crosses, each of which bears four names. The grounds roll across the countryside away from the road. A rare surviving German monument bearing the inscription 'Gott mit Uns' stands over a large mass grave in the rear.

The French ossuary is 3.8 km south of Sommepy-Tahure beside highway D907. (49.218380, 4.542538)

The front lines ran across the Souain-Sommepy road at the French **Ossuaire de la Ferme de Navarin**, the site of ferocious combat. The pyramidal structure holds the remains of 10,000 unidentified soldiers who died in the epic Champagne battles as well as the body of général Henri Gourand, commander of the French Fourth Army in Champagne, who was interred here in 1948. Three larger-than-life military figures top the monument; the soldier carrying a machine gun on the right is in American uniform and was modeled after Lieutenant Quentin Roosevelt. The ground behind the ossuary still retains faint impressions of trenches and craters. The ossuary is open mid-March through September, on Friday and Saturday from 14:00 to 18:00 and on Sunday and holidays from 10:00 to 12:00 and 14:00 to 18:00; 1 November and 11 November from 10:00 to 12:00 and 14:00 to 16:00. No admission charge.

Other Sites of Interest:

A German blockhouse, slightly hidden by recent road reconstruction, remains at the intersection of highways D977 and D220, 200 meters north of the ossuary. (49.222172, 4.544205)

Southeast of Sommepy-Tahure is the Camp Militaire de Suippes. The large, brush-covered tract is an active military base and is closed to civilians; however, guided tours of the destroyed villages and other sites are occasionally offered.

Fifteen kilometers east of Sommepy-Tahure toward Séchault, the **369th** (Harlem Hellfighters) **Regiment**, formerly the 15th New York National Guard Regiment, is commemorated as the first African-American regiment to serve with the American Expeditionary Forces. The nickname 'Hell Fighters' was given to them by the Germans due to their toughness and that they never lost a man through capture or lost a trench or a foot of ground to the enemy. It's soldiers fought in French Divisions receiving French rations and equipment.

Champagne Offensive

Sommepy American Monument atop Blanc Mont; note shell crater in foreground, (left).

An example of the detail that surrounds the monument's observation tower, (below).

Warning sign at Camp Militaire de Suppes identifying it as a Zone Rouge - a restricted area due to unexploded ordinance, (right).

Ossuarie de la Ferme de Navarin detail, (left).

On 30 September, the unit was under German attack and, although twice wounded the previously night and again that morning, 1st Lieutenant George S Robb from Salina, Kansas, remained in command of his platoon. Later that same day a bursting shell added two more wounds and killed his commanding officer and two company officers. Robb assumed command of the company and organized its positions in the trenches. With courage and tenacity, he led his unit forward clearing machine-gun and sniping posts. [25]

The monument is a black granite obelisk with golden English script. It is dedicated to the 93rd Division, 369th Regiment, and 115th Regiment. The opposite side commemorates the 161st French Division. (49.264537, 4.733718)

West of Séchault 1.3 km toward Ardeuil (D6) a narrow, paved road continues 900 meters to a gated monument on the right. Early on the morning of 28 September 1918, Company C, 371st Regiment, was ordered to assault Côte 188, a heavily defended hill overlooking a farm near Ardeuil-et-Montfauxelles. At first, the German defenders offered stiff resistance utilizing mortars, machine guns and steady rifle fire. The advance was not halted, however; with the Americans steadily gaining ground. A German surrender signal proved to be a ruse and machine guns opened up again. Within minutes, the company's strength was reduced by half. Corporal Freddie Stowers became his platoon's senior man.

Stowers successfully led his platoon to the first German trench line and reduced the machine guns by enfilade fire. Stowers then reorganized his force and led a charge against the second German line of trenches. During this assault, Stowers was struck by enemy machine-gun fire, but kept going until struck a second time and collapsed from loss of blood. Inspired by Stowers' courage, the men forged ahead and successfully drove the Germans from the hill and into the plain below.

A stone monument with painted engravings on all four sides honors the **371st Infantry Regiment**, 93rd Division (Colored) and lists the men who died in the assault. The top of the monument suffered damage when it was hit by an artillery shell in World War II. The monument is located near the point where Freddie Stowers won the Medal of Honor and the trenches he attacked are still visible.[26] (49.258207, 4.708868)

St-Mihiel Offensive
12 to 18 September 1918

The Allies planned three great offensives for the fall of 1918 to crush remaining German resistance. The French and Americans would advance through the Argonne Forest toward Mézières and Sedan to cut the main German supply route behind their front lines. The British would advance toward the French frontier at Maubeuge and together with Belgian and French contingents, move toward Ghent in Flanders. Preceding these efforts would be an assault by the American First Army against the 1914-created salient at St-Mihiel, which had been a quiet sector used as

---

25   First Lieutenant George S Robb was awarded the Medal of Honor.

26   Corporal Freddie Stowers, the grandson of a slave from Sandy Springs, South Carolina, was awarded the Medal of Honor in 1991 after a Congress-inspired Defense Department review uncovered the lost recommendation. Stowers is buried in Meuse-Argonne American Cemetery. He was 22 years old.

a training ground for new American divisions before they were sent to other fronts.

The St-Mihiel salient enclosed multiple German defense lines and was anchored across its base by the Michel Line protecting a strategic German lateral rail line that supported troop movements along the Western Front and the Briey coal fields, which were necessary for war production. Seven German divisions had four years to string wire, dig deep dugouts, place machine guns, and range artillery. The relative peacefulness of the sector, however, had bred complacency and many of the German defenders were weak *Landsturm*[27] units.

American units comprised mostly infantry because the rapid manpower increase lacked time to form adequate support units. The Americans relied upon their British and French allies to supply much of the heavy equipment. For example, artillery pieces were of French manufacture with one-half manned by French crews. Thirteen hundred allied aircraft were piloted by British, French, and American airmen. The assigned 267 light tanks were also of French origin, with French or American crews.

The American attack plan assigned the French II Colonial Corps to occupy the enemy in the nose of salient, while three American corps attacked the flanks. The I and IV Corps fell upon the southern face of the salient, intent upon driving north. The V Corps' 26th Division was to close the trap against the salient's east face.

Before becoming aware of the American plans, the German General Staff had ordered evacuation of the salient to shorten their front and release troops for other sectors. Commanders in the salient were ordered to resist until required to withdraw to the strengthened Michel Line in front of Metz. German reserves were held farther back than normal, thereby restricting their use as counterattack troops.

OBJECTIVE	To eliminate the German threat to the flank of the Meuse-Argonne Offensive
FORCES	
ALLIES:	Nine American divisions and five French divisions plus six divisions in reserve, totaling over 600,000 men (General John Pershing)
GERMAN:	Eight line divisions and five reserve divisions of Army Detachment 'C' (Generalleutnant Georg von Fuchs)
RESULT	All objectives were attained and the salient was eliminated.
CASUALTIES	
ALLIES:	1,236 killed; 8,506 wounded and missing
GERMAN:	2,300 killed and wounded; 13,250 taken prisoner
LOCATION	Verdun-sur-Meuse is 270 km east of Paris; St-Mihiel is 36 km south of Verdun

Battle

General Pershing ordered the attack to commence at 05:00 on 12 September after three thousand guns subjected the enemy to a crushing four-hour artillery bombardment. Shrouded in a heavy fog and misty rain, successive waves of American

---

27 *Landsturm:* militia units considered to be of inferior quality.

troops fell upon the enemy's wire entanglements, tossed grenades into dugouts, and rapidly advanced into open country. The American force crushed the shoulders of the salient and the German resistance faltered. Sensing that the enemy was attempting to withdraw, Pershing ordered the assault to continue through that night. The 1st and 26th Divisions closed the escape route before dawn on the second day, by effecting a linkup near Hattonchâtel. The cleanup continued for several days. The German High Command was shocked by American fighting capabilities long thought to be inferior to even mediocre German units. Although the German units were not their best and lacked heavy guns and reserves, the victory was hailed as a great morale builder by the Americans. French and British military leaders remained skeptical considering the casualty rate to be excessive. Almost immediately the Americans started relocating for more difficult challenges in the Argonne.

Battlefield Tour

The tour leaves St-Mihiel to view the 1914-15 battlefields in the Forêt d'Apremont. The woods were the scene of heavy fighting between French and German forces early in the war with the front lines bisecting the forest. Although American forces never engaged the enemy in this area, the Forêt d'Apremont presents the

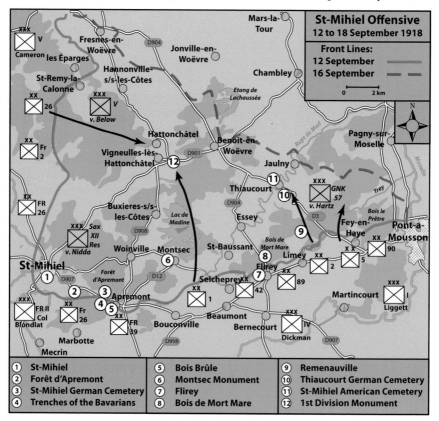

St-Mihiel Offensive

best naturally preserved trenches and dugouts on the Western Front. The site has no re-creations, no artificial preservation, and very few restrictions on entering the actual positions where thousands fought and died amid the melting snow of the winter of 1914 and the spring rains of 1915. We have included the sites in this tour to present the trench warfare experience.

> Leave St-Mihiel southeast toward Apremont-la-Forêt (D907). Turn right toward Ailly-sur-Meuse (D171c) and follow the signs to Bois d'Ailly. A parking area near a monument offers great views down into the Meuse Valley. (48.861676, 5.564977)

Upstream from St-Mihiel, the Meuse curves through a broad valley bordered by wooded hills. The Forêt d'Apremont occupies a plateau east of the river above a 4-kilometer stretch of the valley.

The obelisk near the parking area is dedicated to the units of the **French VIII Corps**, which fought in the Forêt d'Apremont for two years. Its four sides list the numerous regiments who were engaged in the deadly sector.

Battlefield artifacts can be viewed along a short path which runs into the woods parallel to the German lines. The trenches are two meters deep in places, and a large number of underground concrete shelters still stand. Their entrances are barred for safety. Many lead as much as 30 meters below ground, and their stairways descend at very steep angles. The path along the parapet is quite walkable and crosses from side to side as the terrain permits. A more difficult, alternative route is in the actual trenches, where years of fallen leaves now cushion the still muddy tracks. The sounds of mine and grenade explosions and the frenzied shouts of 'gaz!' have been replaced by the chirping of birds and the rustling of dried leaves. The path circles 400 meters through the wood and emerges at the **Monument of the Tranchée de la Soif**.[28] (48.860919, 5.570336)

At 02:00 on 20 May 1915, a company of the French 172nd Regiment commanded by commandant André advanced very quickly within these trenches through five German lines but was trapped by a heavy bombardment that isolated it from supporting units to the rear. André and his eighty soldiers, without food or water amid the May heat and suffocating dust of exploding shells, repelled repeated attacks by Prussian Guards. On 22 May at 18:00, with all their ammunition expended, the sixty-three exhausted survivors were captured and the position became known as *Tranchée de la Soif* or 'trench of thirst.' The stone commemorates the steadfastness of commandant Andre, his men, and all the soldiers of the 172nd and 372nd Regiments.

> Return to the road toward Apremont-la-Forêt (D907) and continue past the motocross course to observe the German first aid bunker on the right. (48.869219, 5.601199)

---

28   For the ardent hiker, signboards give directions for a 20-kilometer *Sentier Historique*, a network of paths that link four major sites within the Forêt d'Apremont and whose routes are marked by orange and yellow signs with a barbed-wire logo. The paths are sometimes difficult to follow; carrying a detailed map of the forest should be considered.

Forêt d'Apremont

Tranchée de la Soif winds through the Forêt d'Apremont, (right).

Remnants of a strategic German first aid bunker alongside the road north of Apremont-le-Forêt, (below).

German gravestones from early in the First World War in German St-Mihiel Cemetery, (left).

Abri d'Allemand in the area known as the Tranchées des Bavarois et de Roffignac, (right).

The road passes a well-constructed and rather extensive **German first aid post** on the right sited below the level of the roadway. Slightly farther ahead, a sign indicates the access road to the **St-Mihiel German Military Cemetery** on the left. The burial ground in the Forêt de Gobessart contains many original German headstones erected early in the war, when the Germans still had hopes of victory. The site is interesting, though the approach road goes through a foreboding abandoned industrial area. (48.877146, 5.607998)

After an additional 1.1 km on the road toward Apremont, turn right into the woods where a Second World War monument stands on the left shoulder. Continue on the unpaved road toward a parking area. (48.859822, 5.615458)

This area is known as the ***Tranchées des Bavarois et de Roffignac*** (Trenches of the Bavarians and the county of Roffignac). The site presents one of the most fantastic First World War trench areas on the Western Front. A large shell crater appears almost immediately upon entering the wood on the right. Approximately 300 meters farther on the left is a French sap entrance. Directions to the 'Abri Allemande' (German outpost) is signed before the parking area. The concrete Bavarian outpost's entrance bears the inscription '*In Treue Fest*' (Firm in Loyalty) — the slogan of Bavarian regiments. Continue to the parking area, where hundreds of meters of German trenches and concrete shelters built around a French salient are easily accessible. Trilingual signs identify and explain their uses and construction. The underbrush has been removed, and the pathways are mostly walkable. Among the strongpoints and shelter entrances are tangled sections of original barbed wire, some still supported upon their pigtail posts. The French first and second line trenches are only 100 meters further. The site offers numerous paths for exploration, a large parking area, and even picnic benches.

Return to highway D907 and continue an additional 1.1 km to an unpaved road on the right. Proceed on that roadway for 550 m to the Bois Brûle signboard. (48.857738,5.625617)

Highway D907, a key German supply line for St-Mihiel, was vulnerable to interdicting fire from French defenses located in these forests. Bavarian troops fought for three months to force the French back 300 meters while suffering 15,000 casualties. The lines eventually stabilized with a mere 50 meters separating the combatants.

The parking lot at the entrance to the **Bois Brûle** contains an orientation table that helps untangle the intermixed trench lines in this complex battlefield. Remnants of French and German trenches are a short distance into the forest. The German trenches are noted for their concrete construction, whereas the French trench walls were supported by wood and thus have almost disappeared.

Montsec is 7.5 km northeast of Apremont-la-Forêt on highway D2; signs indicate the side road to the *Mémorial Américain*. (48.889987, 5.713411)

The scale and scope of a battlefield can usually be best seen from high ground and for St-Mihiel the best location is the **Butte de Montsec**, an isolated hill that rises 130 meters (425 feet) above the surrounding countryside and which becomes an increasingly dominant feature while approaching the small village. The southern side was studded with machine guns and the approach slopes were strung with barbed-wire entanglements. Tunnels bored into Montsec provided defenders with shelter and access to observation posts. A telephone exchange at its base transmitted sightings to batteries camouflaged in nearby woods. Montsec was too strongly defended for troops to attempt a frontal assault. Pershing reasoned that after being cut off from German reserves, the position would surrender. His plan therefore called for the dominant heights to be bypassed by the 1st Division, which would then swing around behind it to establish contact with the charging 26th Division. The height was shrouded by smoke shells to prevent observers from reporting attackers' positions. On 13 September, surrounded by American forces and according to Pershing's plan, the Germans abandoned Montsec. Almost exactly 26 years later, Americans were again fighting Germans over Montsec. On 2 September 1944, American forces fired upon a German machine gun position on the hill.

Today the butte is crowned with the **Montsec American Monument** consisting of a circular colonnade surrounding a bronze relief battlefield map that indicates the various unit locations. The full scope of I and IV Corps' 14-mile attack front can be seen stretching from east of Thiaucourt on the left as marked by its church steeple to Seicheprey on the right. The huge Lac de Madine was lowland in 1918 and has since been flooded to support water sports and recreational activities. The monument is always open; no admission charge.

> From Montsec continue southeast for 6.5 km to the church in the center of Seicheprey (D119, then unnamed road). (48.869498, 5.790981)

The road passes through the village of Seicheprey, which was the scene of a German raid in the early morning of 20 April 1918 against the 102nd Regiment, 26th 'Yankee' Division. The attack was the first major assault by German forces and was designed to test the newly arrived American troops. Behind a rolling artillery barrage, 1,200 German assault troops cut off seven platoons in the frontline trenches, flanked the town, and captured the village. Hand-to-hand fighting raged in the narrow confines of Seicheprey before the attackers retired with 136 prisoners leaving 160 dead. Both sides claimed victory. A now-unused water fountain, which was presented to the village by the people of Connecticut, the home of many of the Yankee division soldiers, is beside the church

> Flirey is 5 km east of Seicheprey on highway (D958).

The front line of American 42nd and 89th Divisions was along the left side of the road. A bronze tablet affixed to a block plinth across from the Flirey church displays two doughboys victoriously standing over a German helmet and gas canister commemorating the **American Army's First Offensive**. The side of the memorial commemorates the American divisions which participated in the actions in the sector

St-Mihiel Offensive

American gun crew firing upon Montsec, (right). NARA
Montsec American Memorial, (below),

Front lines near Sommedieue, (below). NARA

Thiaucourt-Regniéville War Memorial, (below); St-Mihiel American Cemetery, (below right).

from Flirey to Thiaucourt-Regniéville. [29](48.875069, 5.847380)

East of the town center and upon a hillock on the right are the ruins of the old church, left in its partially destroyed state to mark the position of the original village and to commemorate local dead. (48.875925, 5.851123)

Bois de Mort Mare is accessed north of Flirey from the road toward Essey (D904). A monument along the road remembers French casualties in the mine warfare that occurred from February 1915 to April 1917, when the French and Germans sought dominance in the large forest. (48.885489, 5.845083) The wood retains craters from mines detonated in the vicious struggle as well as a few stretches of poorly defined trenches. (48.885489, 5.845083)

From Flirey, continue east 4.0 km toward Pont à Mousson (D958) then turn left toward Remenauville (D75) and continue to the **2nd Division** boulder at the bottom of the valley which identifies the unit's 12 September start line. (48.896565, 5.899301).
Continue 900 m to the small parking area and walk into the forest. (48.901996, 5.907989)

The destroyed and abandoned village of **Remenauville** (population 138) had been occupied by the Germans since 1914 and its position on the front line all but assured its destruction. The 2nd Division captured it on 12 September.

The original church has been replaced by a small chapel, where signs describe the village before the war. From the memorial chapel a short walk leads along the narrow streets of the prewar French village, where now only scrub brush and vines occupy the sites of a butcher's or a farmer's home as identified by small placards.

Continue on highway D75 to the intersection with highway D3. (48.910378, 5.927843)

The intersection is studded with memorial stones; one, identified by the red diamond symbol, marks the starting point of the **5th Division's** assault upon Thiaucourt. A second plaque states that the same division passed through this area in September 1944 on its way to the Moselle River after fighting 1,100 km from the Normandy Beaches. [30] (48.910430, 5.927912)

Nearby a **Demarcation Stone** marks the limit of the 1918 German advance. (48.910155, 5.927987)

Proceed toward Thiaucourt-Regniéville on highway D3.

---

29   Pilot Sergeant Lee Duncan, 135th Observation Squadron, sighted a puppy wandering amid the rubble of what once was Flirey. He landed, rescued the animal, and requested permission to accept a German shepherd pup as the squadron's mascot. Duncan allowed a German PoW to train the dog and brought it home after the war. In 1919 an accidental meeting with Darryl Zanuck in Hollywood led to the first feature film starring a dog that became famous in theater and television — Rintintin.

30   The 5th Division erected 27 such monuments across the battlefields where it fought. Several of these locations are noted in the text.

A **German machine-gun blockhouse**, which defended the roadway, remains in excellent condition despite the noticeable damage at its base caused by an artillery shell. The approach to Thiaucourt presents an example of the rolling hills and encroaching forests typical of the St-Mihiel battlefield. (48.929210, 5.901680)

Near Thiaucourt, the road passes the enormous **Thiaucourt-Regniéville German Cemetery** on the left. The cemetery is accessible from old highway D3c. The cemetery contains 11,685 graves, a collection of private memorials in its northeast corner, and a special section with burials from the Franco-Prussian War. (48.945897, 5.877457)

Thiaucourt, an important German supply depot, was captured by the 2nd Division at approximately 09:00 on 12 September along with a vast quantity of German war matériel. An imposing **War Memorial** in the town center adjacent to the church depicts the unity of French and American soldiers. The names of the men of Thiaucourt who died for France and of the American divisions who had a part in the delivery of the town are engraved on the monument in gold plate letters. The American soldier on the War Memorial is modeled after Captain Oliver Cunningham.[31] The exterior walls of the church and the Hôtel-de-Ville still show damage from shell splinters. (48.954027, 5.865494)

Continue north toward Verdun (D3) for 1.1 km to the cemetery on the left. (48.956939, 5.852319)

St-Mihiel American Cemetery
Route de Verdun, 54470 Thiaucourt
Tel: +33 (0)3 83 80 01 01
See introduction for hours and website.

St-Mihiel is the third largest of the First World War American Cemeteries in Europe and holds 4,153 dead, many from the St-Mihiel action. An American eagle tops a sundial located at the intersection of the tree-lined walks that divide the cemetery into four plots and its plinth bears the inscription: 'Time shall not dim the glory of their deeds.' A chapel, peristyle, and map building occupy the south end of the cemetery. The wall lists the names of 284 soldiers whose graves were never located. The rear terrace overlooks the ground over which the 89th and 42nd Divisions advanced. The American Monument on Montsec is visible in the distance.

Continue northwest 12.2 km (D3, becomes, D67, D904, D901) to the roundabout east of Vigneulles-lès-Hattonchâtel. (48.978483, 5.715075)

---

31   Captain Oliver Cunningham, an only son from Evanston, Illinois and cum laude graduate of Yale University, served as a lieutenant in the 15th Field Artillery Regiment, 2nd Division. He fought at Château-Thierry, Vaux, Belleau Wood, and St-Mihiel. His captain's commission arrived on the day after he was killed by mortar fire on his 24th birthday. Cunningham was awarded both the Distinguished Service Cross and the Silver Star Medal. The Thiaucourt church was reconstructed after the war by his parents as a remembrance of their son. The location of Cunningham's death remains preserved and cared by the local residents in the forest one mile east of Jaulny. (48.9734 5.898811)

The **1st Division Memorial** marks the junction between the two American forces, thus eliminating the salient. The unit memorial lists the names of the 98 killed; wounded and missing totaled 489.

> Continue into Vigneulles-lès-Hattonchâtel (D908) to place Taylor across from the Hôtel-de-Ville. (48.980803, 5.703808)

The French war memorial bears a statue remembering 1st Lieutenant Moses Taylor, Jr. On 23 March 1918 Taylor, a member of the 2nd Division, assembled twenty volunteers for a raid in no man's land. The objective was to capture a mill housing several German machine guns. With Taylor in command, the group went over the top at 02:00 and crept toward the German lines, moving through a stream and across a field of old corn stalks. Taylor was shot by a German who emerged from what looked like a freshly dug trench. It was impossible to recover Taylor's body at the time because an artillery barrage was laid down on the area. It was not until two weeks later that the company finally took the German trench. Taylor had been taken to a German hospital where he later died. The Germans buried him in Vigneulles. Taylor's wealthy parents made significant contributions to rebuild the war-devastated town. [32]

> Exit Vigneulles toward Hattonchâtel (D179).

The ridgetop village of Hattonchâtel has a one-way loop road and includes some marvelous old buildings and stunning views east onto the Woëvre Plain. Steps go down and round behind the church, erected in 1328, for fantastic views of the countryside. (48.992064, 5.704110)

Meuse-Argonne Offensive
26 September to 11 November 1918

Pershing's quarrels with Foch over dispersing American troops into French and British battalions resulted in a compromise by which the neophyte American First Army would undertake two offensives within two weeks on battlefields 100 kilometers apart. The American logistics team, headed by Lieutenant Colonel George Marshall, having resoundingly completed the first task at St-Mihiel, prepared for the second.[33]

The attack targeted the most critical point of the German railroad transportation network at Sedan. Loss of this choke point would separate the German armies in the north from those in the south and would make supply or withdrawal of German forces from Flanders nearly impossible. Recognizing the Argonne's strategic importance, the Germans strengthened the area with several defensive lines which formed an almost continuous, 16-kilometer-wide belt of machine guns, barbed wire, and dugouts. The terrain provided numerous opportunities for gun emplacements with

---

32 First Lieutenant Moses Taylor Jr is buried in Meuse-Argonne American Cemetery. He was twenty years old.

33 General George C Marshal was US Army Chief of Staff during the Second World War. He later became Secretary of State and the driving force behind the Marshall Plan to rebuild destroyed economies after the war. He was awarded the Nobel Peace Prize in 1953 for those efforts.

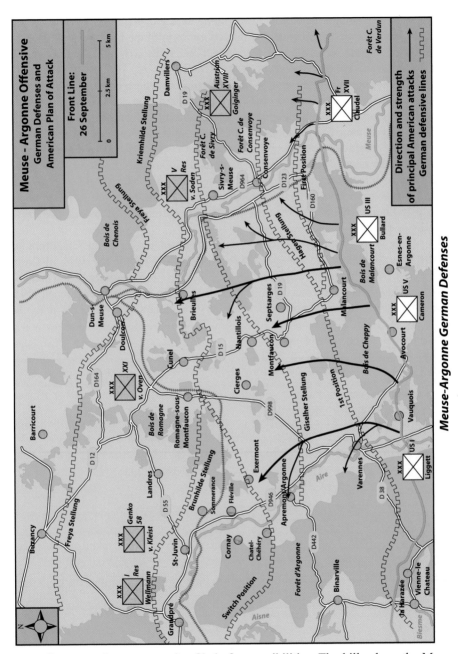

Meuse - Argonne Offensive
German Defenses and
American Plan of Attack

Front Line:
26 September

0   2.5 km   5 km

Direction and strength
of principal American attacks
German defensive lines

Meuse-Argonne German Defenses

mutually supporting cross- and enfilade-fire possibilities. The hills along the Meuse valley and the wooded plateau of the Forêt d'Argonne provided excellent artillery positions, and the center of the battlefield was dominated by the Butte de Montfaucon.

Preparations required the movement of over 800,000 men and related matériel. Even before the St-Mihiel operation had ceased, American infantrymen were moving north on three narrow roads hiding during daylight to preserve secrecy. Forward positions were maintained by French troops until the last minute to hide the presence of American troops on the front line. Some units arrived at the jumping-off trenches just hours before the assault.

The American success at St-Mihiel could have been partially attributed to German plans for evacuation; however, the same could not be said about the Argonne. In the three years after the boiling battles against the French had quieted to a steady simmer, the Germans had developed the dense woods and steep buttes into killing fields. Enemy positions were so strong that général Pétain opined that the Americans should consider taking Montfaucon by Christmas as good progress. German defensive lines, named after characters in Wagnerian operas, culminated in the *Kriemhilde Stellung,* which ran from Brieulles through Romagne-sous-Montfaucon to Grandpré – 12 to 15 kilometers north of the start line. Farther north, past the incomplete *Freya Stellung,* the fields were generally open.

Three corps of the American First Army moved abreast along a line from the Meuse River on the east to the edges of the Forêt d'Argonne on the west; III Corps on the right, V Corps in the center, I Corps on the left – each with three divisions up front and one division in reserve. To the east across the Meuse River, French XVII Corps' objective was to silence German artillery positioned on the heights along the east bank. West of the Argonne the French Fourth Army was to engage the enemy in a coordinated drive on Sedan.

OBJECTIVE	To cut German transportation routes around Sedan as part of a coordinated allied offensive.
FORCES	
ALLIES:	Nine American divisions and four French divisions plus six divisions in reserve; 384 aircraft and 215 tanks (General John Pershing)
GERMAN:	Army Group C initially with five divisions eventually growing to twenty divisions (General der Artillerie Max Karl von Gallwitz)
RESULT	The defensive lines were penetrated and the American advance continued until the Armistice.
CASUALTIES	
AMERICAN:	26,277 killed, 95,786 wounded, and over 26,000 taken prisoner
GERMAN:	28,000 killed and 92,250 wounded
LOCATION	Verdun-sur-Meuse is 270 km east of Paris; Montfaucon is 33 km northwest of Verdun

Battle

At 02:30 on 26 September, 2,775 guns opened a three-hour bombardment along the 40-kilometer front. The duration of the artillery preparation was purposely short to minimize early enemy reinforcement. The infantry followed behind the rolling barrage into the densely woven fabric of ravines, gun emplacements, machine-gun nests, trenches, and wire entanglements. A heavy fog hid some German strongpoints, which were bypassed. On the first day, I Corps moved swiftly along the Aire Valley but advanced only 1.6 km in the dense woods of the Argonne. V Corps drove past the left of Montfaucon, and III Corps did the same on the strongpoint's right, leaving the height as a salient in American lines. Although Montfaucon was captured by noon on 27 September, the delay allowed the Germans to reinforce positions to its north and end America's hopes of a quick attack upon the main line of resistance. By the end of the third day, *Hagen* and *Giselher Stellung* had been penetrated after a 10-kilometer advance and American troops faced the *Kriemhilde Stellung*. Increased German resistance, supported by the transfer of seven fresh, first-class divisions and improved artillery support, forced a brief halt in the assault. Pershing admitted that the American Expeditionary Force was 'now committed to a direct frontal attack against strong enemy forces.' Hopes for a quick exploitation were replaced with a battle of attrition.

The American advance, however, combined with British, French, and Belgian offensives elsewhere along the Western Front had sealed Germany's fate. On 3 October, Hindenburg wrote, 'There is now no longer any possibility of forcing peace on the enemy.'

Pershing replaced tired units with fresh divisions and engineers constructed plank roads to cross the morass of no man's land. The assault was renewed on 4 October. The Germans were experts at using the terrain for defense and each meter of progress was resisted by machine-gun fire and well-sited artillery. The batteries on the heights of the Meuse were especially deadly to American troops on the right flank. On 5 October, Pershing ordered the French XVII Corps to attack those positions to relieve the pressure upon the III Corps. On 8 October, a stunning attack from the Aire valley west of Châtel-Chéhéry by the 28th and 82nd 'All American' Divisions and coordinated with the 77th Division coming up through the forest forced the Germans to abandon the Argonne for fear of being surrounded. The next day, French and American divisions drove the Germans from the hills east of the Meuse ending much of the flank fire.

On 14 October, after a two-day respite, the main *Kriemhilde* Line came under assault. The German forces had increased to forty divisions, but they were unable to stop the relentless attacks. Despite bringing units from other battlefields along the Western Front to stem the advance strongpoints fell in succession after bitter and costly fighting and the last defensive line was breached.

A brief period of recuperation and replacement preceded a two-hour artillery bombardment and assault on 1 November. A rapid advance caused the German High Command to issue orders for a general withdrawal to the east of the Meuse River. The 5th Division established bridgeheads across the river at Dun-sur-Meuse on 4 November. By 7 November, units of I Corps were on the heights above Sedan and achieved the ultimate objective of cutting the German rail lines around that city. The battle ended with the Armistice of 11 November – ending the greatest American military effort to that time.

Battlefield Tour

The Meuse-Argonne battlefield is bordered by the unfordable Meuse River to the east and the almost impenetrable Forêt d'Argonne to the west. The broad farming valley in between contained the slow-flowing Aire River. In the center of the battlefield

Meuse-Argonne Offensive

A German howitzer battery in the Argonne during July 1917, (left). NARA

US 77th Division resting during advance among the shattered stumps in the Argonne Forest, (right). NARA

Congested roadways slowed the American advance; this image was taken in Esnes, (left). NARA

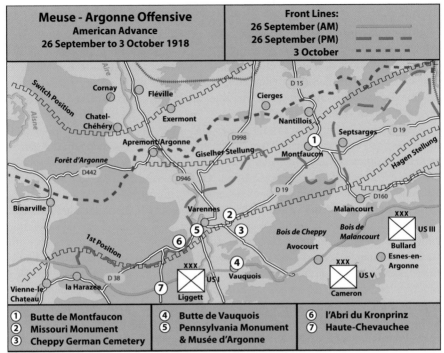

Meuse-Argonne Offensive Phase 1

was an elevation known as Montfaucon. The great German-French struggle of 1915 had hardened into a front line, which cut the Argonne in half along a line running east-west from Vauquois through the forest to the valley of the Biesme River.

Since the Meuse-Argonne battlefield covers 1,500 square kilometers, the tour focuses on select locations critical to the initial success of the offensive. The countryside is dotted with divisional memorials erected after the war, each having its own distinctive design and many of them are passed along the way.

Leave Verdun-sur-Meuse north toward Varennes-en-Argonne along the west bank of the river. Turn west onto highway D19 and follow into Montfaucon. From Forges to Malancourt the road travels along the valley of the Forges River, and the ridgeline to the left held the American front on the morning of 26 September. Continue to the place du Général Pershing in the center of Montfaucon. (49.271851, 5.133314)

The **'Sammies' Memorial** features a white marble plaque with gold leaf text in French mounted on a granite stone base to honor the American soldiers, who served in the area during the Meuse-Argonne Offensive in September 1918.

From the village of Montfaucon, follow the signs to the *Monument Américain*. (49.272080, 5.141918)

Montfaucon was originally the site of an ancient monastery reported to have been the scene of a great battle in 888 AD against Norman invaders. It witnessed additional struggles in the Hundred Years War, the Religious Wars of the 16th century, and the passage of Prussian troops on their way to the Battle of Valmy in 1792. The village of Montfaucon, which grew around the monastery, was obliterated during the four years of the First World War; however, the monastery ruins were a key observation post for the *Giselher Stellung* and was thus developed into a veritable fortress of above- and underground positions.

At 11:00 on 26 September, the 37th Division emerged from the Bois Malancourt and entered trench systems to the north. The first assault upon Montfaucon started at 18:00 reaching the lower slopes of the hill, but the advance halted at nightfall. The assault renewed at dawn in a driving rainstorm while two American divisions attacked from the front and right flank. By noon the hill was cleared.

The **Montfaucon American Monument** is a 55-meter Doric column topped with the figure of Liberty, erected to commemorate the American First Army's victory in the Meuse-Argonne. It faces the American start line of 26 September. Observation rooms with splendid views over much of the battlefield as well as a table of orientation are accessed via 234 steps or an elevator. Montfaucon is in the center of the American battlefield and can be seen from various points during the tour. Open every weekday throughout the year and on weekends from 1 July through 15 September from 09:00 to 17:00; closed 25 December and 1 January. No admission charge.

The ruins of the **Abbey of Montfaucon**, founded by a seventh century monk, are directly behind the American Monument. Incorporated into the monastery walls is a German concrete blockhouse which was used as on observation post. The grounds around the church contain several additional wartime structures that were built during the four-year occupation of the village. Paths through the underbrush provide access, and a brief survey of the area demonstrates the strength of the position, even though vegetation now blocks views of the surrounding countryside. (49.273132, 5.141415)

Leave Montfaucon southwest toward Cheppy / Varennes-en-Argonne (D19). After 8.6 km, pause at the monument on the left. (49.225013, 5.056030)

The **Missouri Monument**'s elevated platform displays a granite plinth topped with an Angel of Victory holding an olive wreath. It was erected by the State of Missouri to commemorate its sons who fought in the war, many of them members of the 35th Division, formed from the Missouri and Kansas National Guard, which advanced through this area. In nearby woods Battery D, 129th Field Artillery, commanded by then-captain and future United States President Harry S Truman, was laying down artillery fire. During the second day of the assault, Truman spotted enemy artillery repositioning such as to fire upon neighboring American troops. Truman, against specific orders to not divulge his position, opened fire and scattered the German unit. Surprisingly, he was not court-martialed for disobeying his orders.

Also near Cheppy, the fledgling American Tank Corp took the field manning small, two-man, French Renault tanks. The unit was under command of an ex-cavalry officer then-Major George Patton, Jr. Patton's 142-tank unit charged up the Aire River

Montfaucon

Monastery ruins atop
Butte de Montfaucon, (above)

Montfaucon American
Monument, (right).

Ruins of
Montfaucon
village church,
(left) NARA.

Missouri
Monument
in Cheppy,
(right).

Valley on the first day of battle. Patton, impatient for reports on the unit's progress, left his command post to view his unit by following tank tracks forward. Finding his unit's

progress blocked at a ditch crossing, Patton personally directed the work crews while under enemy artillery fire. At one point, feeling the work progressing too slowly, Patton hit one of the men on the head with a shovel. After crossing the ditch, Patton led a group of six volunteers forward to silence enemy machine guns saying 'To hell with them. They can't hit me.' Five of the men were killed, Patton was wounded, and for him the war was over.

The **Cheppy German Military Cemetery** is on an unnamed minor road 1.4 km southeast of the village. The cemetery sits upon the ridge crest between Cheppy and the Butte de Vauquois. The cemetery's 6,165 graves are marked by iron crosses bearing four names per cross. (49.227351, 5.070661)

Colonel George S Patton Jr. (NARA)

From Cheppy proceed south 7.4 km to Vauquois. Upon entering the village, note the French memorial on the left which states: 'From here on 28.02.1915 the [French] 45th Infantry Regiment launched an assault on Vauquois.' Follow rue d'Orléans up the hillside on the right to the parking area. (49.205595, 5.070139)

The **Butte de Vauquois** is 4 kilometers east of the Argonne Plateau and rises 70 meters to dominate the Aire valley. The Germans captured the site on 24 September 1914 and the hilltop village of 168 people was suddenly on the front lines. Preliminary French assaults in October and December failed to gain any strategic footing because German artillery in Bois de Cheppy applied flanking fire. Until February 1915, French infantry assaults were essentially sacrifices of men due to the lack of artillery support.

The French 10th Division assaulted Vauquois on 17 February, starting with the explosion of four small mines. Waves of attacks continued until 4 March when they were able to establish themselves on the crest of the hill. With each side controlling one half of the old village, the front lines were only 9 meters apart at certain places. Surface positions became so deadly that the underground 'war of the mines' commenced. Digging new tunnels and exploding mines under enemy positions continued until August 1917; by then the subterranean galleries were so deep that getting sufficiently large explosions became impractical and the mine warfare essentially ceased.

Amis de Vauquois et de sa Région
1, rue d'Orléans, 55270 Vauquois
Tel: +33 (0)3 29 88 46 49
Email: amis.vauquois@wanadoo.fr
Web: http://butte-vauquois.fr/en/

The site is open to visitors at all times; however, tours of the tunnel system are offered by the volunteers only on the first Sunday of each month from 09:30 to 12:00 and on 1 May and 8 May at 10:00 and 18:00 and in September during 'Heritage Days.'

There is a slight fee for a guided tour. A small museum is adjacent to the parking area.

From the parking area, walk through the French communications trench passed several of the French tunnel entrances. The rusted iron spikes strewn about once held barbed-wired entanglements, portions of which remain in the undergrowth. The butte has been frequently described as a giant termite nest, containing kilometers of galleries and hundreds of chambers – some reaching 100 meters below the surface. The contours of the hill have been reshaped by 519 explosions and it is now several meters lower than in 1914. The prewar village was completely obliterated, and nothing remains except a few scattered stones that mark the site of the village church.

At the edge of the field of craters along what once was the village's main street the **Lanterne des Morts** commemorates the soldiers killed fighting on the hill. The lantern also marks the furthest French advance of February and March 1915. The lantern is lit on special days, including 26 September to commemorate the beginning of the Meuse-Argonne Offensive. A table of orientation describes the 'war of the mines' and its geographic relationship to the village. The largest crater, on the western side of the hill, measures 80 meters across. It was formed on 14 May 1916, when a German detonation of 50,000 kilograms of explosives destroyed a French dugout, killing its 108 inhabitants. Views to the north show Cheppy, Montfaucon, and other sites of the Meuse-Argonne Offensive.

A walk down into the craters and up the far side approaches '*Feste Petsch*' the German trench system where a restored trench can be entered to view a sniper's firing step and other trench construction details.

Continue west (D212) to highway (D946) and follow to the low stone monument on the right in Neuvilly. (49.16111 5.05806)

A white stone shard with a bronze plaque, erected in 2008 as a symbol of Franco-American cooperation, remembers the destruction of Neuvilly during the war and the fighting spirit of the 28th and 35th Divisions, which contributed to the liberation of the Aire Valley, Vauquois, and Varennes-en-Argonne.

Reverse direction to Varennes-en-Argonne crossing the bridge over the Aire River and continue on rue Louis XVI to the large memorial plaza on the right. (49.225584, 5.032459)

Pennsylvania Monument in Varennes-en-Argonne

The double colonnade of the impressive **Pennsylvania Monument** dominates a large park to commemorate the men of

Butte de Vauquois

Aerial view of explosion craters on Butte de Vauquois; note opposing trench lines to the left and right of the craters, (above). NARA

Lanterne des Morts on the Butte de Vauquois, (above).

German trench on the Butte de Vauquois, (right). NARA

Reconstructed French trench on the Butte de Vauquois, (left).

Pennsylvania's 28th 'Keystone' Division which captured the area west of the Aire.

Musée d'Argonne
Rue Louis XVI, 55270 Varennes-en-Argonne
Tel: + 33 (0)3 29 80 71 14
E-mail: mairievarennesenargonne@wanadoo.fr
Web: http://tourisme-argonne-1418.fr/musee-largonne/

Open weekdays 19 April through 30 June from 15:00 to 18:00; daily July through September from 10:30 to 12:00 and 14:30 to 18:00. Fee.

Adjacent to the monument, the museum is dedicated to the history of the area. The lower floor contains displays relating to the First World War and describing American and Italian participation. Dioramas of the mine warfare are included along with several original German trench maps. Although most of the signs are not in English, the displays are self-explanatory. (49.225158, 5.031646)

Other Sites of Interest:
Highway D38 west of Varennes roughly marks the start lines of the Meuse-Argonne Offensive in this sector. The area had seen sharp fighting between French and German troops in 1915 and holds several sites pertaining to that conflict.

> Leave Varennes-en-Argonne west toward Vienne le Château (D38), after 3.0 km turn right onto an unnamed, pot-holed side road and proceed 650 m into the forest. Four ruined structures are not visible from the road but are signed. (48.644444, 6.679722)

After the front line stabilized during the first months of the war, several shelters were built as advanced Command Posts for the generals and officers of the German Army staff commanded by Kronprinz Rupprecht of Bavaria.[34] One such structure, known as **l'Abri du Kronprinz**, was built in these woods only two kilometers from the front lines. The naturally strong site was hidden from observation by dense forest and built into the side of the hill. Each building was protected by a 6-meter-thick concrete roof layered with metal beams and railroad sleepers and connected by trenches. They were also noted for their opulence being lit by electricity, heated by traditional large Bavarian stoves while surrounded outside by flower beds. The rooms were paneled with walnut and furniture, from opulent local houses, included ice cabinets, hot tubs, and bowling alleys. Officers drank fine wines and schnapps.

The structures remain, stripped of their finery decades ago, but still representative of their strong construction. Access is unimpeded, and the ground can be explored where the very deep shell craters suggest that the abris were subjected to some near misses. Communication trenches link the structures and remain 6-feet deep even after years of leaves and debris washed in by the rain. The Kronprinz's personal shelter is identified by its bay window with half cupola.

---

34 After the war Kronprinz Rupprecht of Bavaria retreated to Wieringen Island, the Netherlands where he lived in luxurious exile until his death in 1951.

> Return to highway D38 continuing toward Vienne; after 650 m turn left onto Haute Chevauchée. Continue on this lonely, but scenic, forest road as it runs along the top of a north-south ridge and forms the backbone of the Argonne plateau. Ravines that cut into the plateau are visible to the left and right, and these were frequently the sites of desperate fighting. After 2.4 km, pass the Ossuaire de la Haute Chevauchée to its parking area on the left. (49.189105, 4.994069)

For much of the war, the front line crossed the highway near this point. Weary of the massive casualties that the attacks of July and September 1915 produced, the Germans and French resorted to mine warfare. Although casualties decreased, the front lines hardly moved.

From the parking area, a gentle path follows the old French communications trench to approach Côte 285, the highest point on the Haute Chevauchée and upon which stands the **Monument Ossuaire de la Haute-Chevauchée**, the major French memorial to the Argonne fighting. The monument presents a nine-meter limestone pillar topped with the bust of a soldier whose hands clasp the handle of a sword overlaying a cross. The names of 275 French regiments which participated in the battles are recorded on its sides; also included are lists of Italian, Czech, and American units. Entombed within the ossuary are the remains of 20,000 French soldiers who were killed in the Argonne from 1914 to 1918.

Immediately behind the ossuary is a 50-meter-diameter crater, which was the result of a 52-metric-ton German mine explosion under a French dugout on 12 December 1916. This crater is the largest of a string of similar craters that runs 3.5 kilometers along La Fille Morte to the edge of the Argonne plateau. They were formed during the mine warfare from October 1915 to June 1916 when this sector experienced 223 underground explosions.

The path curves around the north edge of the large crater, and the German first line is clearly indicated off to the left. One can see the narrow separation between opposing trenches. An Art Deco cross commemorates the 150,000 soldiers of all nations who died in the Argonne from 1914 to 1918. The path then continues through the replanted forest to a viewpoint from which the Lantern Tower on the Butte de Vauquois is visible. Multilingual signboards along the way explain warfare in this area. The path circles back below the rim of the craters, through the German trenches, and across the Haute Chevauchée to the **Kaiser Tunnel**. (49.190424, 4.991848)

After the last major attack of 27 September 1915, the French retained Côte 285 and the ability to fire into German-held ravines. As a consequence, starting in November 1915 German infantry dug what became known as the Kaiser Tunnel to provide access to the front without exposure to French fire. The tunnel was twice expanded and became a major installation, with kilometers of galleries, storage facilities, a hospital, power station, and its own communications exchange. The tunnels were abandoned and their entrances destroyed by the Germans in September 1918. The tunnels are currently closed to visitors, but a virtual tour is available at https://largonnealheure1418.wordpress.com/2014/11/19/kaiser-tunnel/ (French only). A walk in the nearby ravine presents numerous shell craters and trench lines in their unreconstructed state as examples of defenses in the difficult Argonne terrain.

Haute Chevauchée

Abri du Kronprinz
as it appeared
after the war, (left) NARA
and as it appears today,
(above).

French Cimetière
Nationale de la Forestière, (above).

Monument Ossuaire
de la Haute-Chevauchée, (left).

Continue south for 2.9 km to the **French Cimetière Nationale de la Forestière** at the junction with a forest road to Lachalade. Planted between each of its 2,200 graves are hydrangea bushes, for which the cemetery is noted and which present a spectacular display when in bloom. The cemetery is carved out of the woods and remains surrounded by deep forest. The grave plots are perfectly centered on the flagpole and slightly behind the flagpole is a large stone cross. (49.167509, 5.002456)

> Return to Varennes-en-Argonne and proceed north toward Apremont (D38a).

The road travels along the eastern edge of the Argonne forest and crosses the paths of 28th and 35th Divisions in the beginning of the offensive. From Apremont the narrow road toward Binarville (D442) is the only lateral route across the forest and the heavily defended Le Chêne Tondu where a strong German second position had been organized along a ridge and across the Argonne in a direction approximately at right angles to this road. Le Chêne Tondu was the scene of prolonged and intense fighting by the 28th Division for ten days from 28 September until its capture was finally completed in an attack on the morning of 7 October.

> After 2.5 km, stop at a 2-foot-high, plain white stone cross with an inscribed Cross Pattée beside the road. (49.256410, 4.967486)

Apremont German Military Cemetery

A brick sidewalk provides entrance to the **Apremont German Military Cemetery** whose periphery is identified by stone gateposts. The cemetery holds 1,111 German burials, but more interesting are the individual commemorations, many erected when it still appeared that Germany would win the war and the particularly stunning oak and pecan trees among the graves. For example, toward the rear a memorial remembers the scion of a Prussian military family '*Freiherr von Müllenheim-Rechberg, Major und camerade die Jäger ... Gefallen April 8, 1916 Argonne Hohe 285*' – Argonne Hill 285, where the French Ossuary is now located.

> Continue 4.1 km west of the German cemetery, toward Binarville (highway D442 becomes D66) to the small stone beside the road on the west side of the forest. (49.251396, 4.914700)

A simple roadside stele marks the location of the '**Lost Battalion**' and identifies the various units that comprised the composite unit: Companies A, B, C, E,

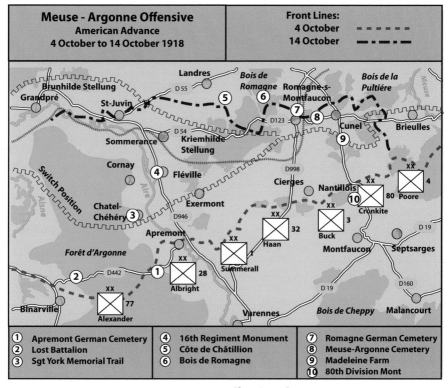

Meuse - Argonne Offensive
American Advance
4 October to 14 October 1918

Front Lines:
4 October – – – – –
14 October – ● – ● – ●

①	Apremont German Cemetery	④	16th Regiment Monument	⑦	Romagne German Cemetery
②	Lost Battalion	⑤	Côte de Châtillion	⑧	Meuse-Argonne Cemetery
③	Sgt York Memorial Trail	⑥	Bois de Romagne	⑨	Madeleine Farm
				⑩	80th Division Mont

Meuse-Argonne Offensive Phase 2

G and H, 308th Regiment; Company K, 307th Regiment; Companies C and D, 306th Machine Gun Battalion — all from the 77th Division. A second memorial, inaugurated on the 90th Anniversary of the events, stands with an informational panel 650 meters ahead. (49.250853, 4.906761)

On 2 October 1918, the 1st Battalion, 308th Regiment, 77th Division, led by Major Charles Whittlesey, a graduate of Harvard Law School from Florence, Wisconsin, was ordered to advance in the dense Argonne Forest and attack Moulin Charleveaux which was held by the German Reserve Infantry Regiment Nr 76. Neighboring units failed to move forward and, as Whittlesey approached his objective, his 670 men became cut off and surrounded in dense woods on a hillside

Roadside marker indicating the location of the Lost Battalion

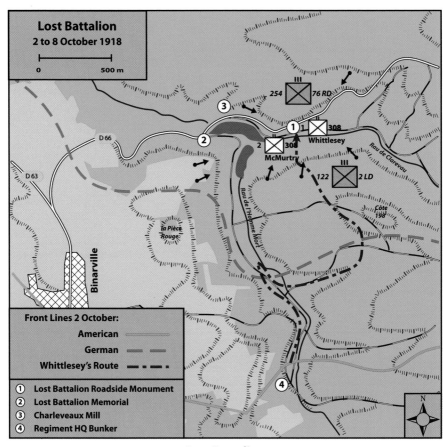

Lost Battalion

below this German-held roadway. The unit became known as The Lost Battalion.

By the second day, Whittlesey had lost 222 men, machine-gun crews were at half strength, and his three medics had exhausted their supply of bandages. Attempts to send reinforcements were beaten back. Supplies dropped by aircraft landed in enemy hands.[35]

Under almost constant artillery and machine-gun fire, Whittlesey sent a message via carrier pigeon, requesting artillery support. Unfortunately, his coordinates were either incorrect or misinterpreted and American artillery shells fell upon their own men. His last carrier pigeon, named Cher Ami, carried the message, 'Our own

---

35   First Lieutenant Harold Ernest Goettler of Chicago, Illinois, with his observer, 2nd Lieutenant Erwin R Bleckley, 50th Aero Squadron, left their airdrome late in the afternoon of 6 October on their second trip to drop supplies to the Lost Battalion. Despite having been subjected to violent enemy fire during an earlier attempt, they flew lower to get the supplies more precisely on target. In the course of the mission the plane was brought down by enemy rifle and machine-gun fire from the ground, resulting in the deaths of Goettler and Bleckley. Both men were awarded the Medal of Honor. Lieutenant Goettler, 28, was returned for burial in Chicago; Lieutenant Bleckley, 23, of Wichita, Kansas, remains buried in Meuse-Argonne American Cemetery.

artillery is dropping a barrage directly on us. For heaven's sake stop it!' Cher Ami flew up into the enemy artillery fire and, despite being shot in the chest, delivered its message.

For six days the men resisted every effort by the enemy to capture the position. Whittlesey and his second in command Captain George McMurtry were both wounded. German surrender demands were ignored. In the end, American forces were able to reach the Lost Battalion, but only 194 of its 670 men walked out unscathed. Their foxholes and shell craters remain, now almost lost among the shrubs and brush on the steep hillside below the roadside marker.[36]

> Return to Apremont and follow highway D42 to the Mairie in Châtel-Chéhéry. (49.282049, 4.953917)

A great single act of bravery took place in the rolling hills west of Châtel-Chéhéry. During an advance, the men of Company G, 328th Regiment, 82nd Division came under the fire of enemy machine guns in sparse woodlands. Seventeen men were ordered to infiltrate the German lines and eliminate the guns.

The men captured a German headquarters before coming under fire from the hillside above. Nine of the seventeen quickly became casualties leaving one-time conscientious objector Corporal Alvin York as the senior man. Leaving the rest of the contingent to guard the prisoners, York crept around enemy positions until six German soldiers left a trench to attack him. York fired all the rounds in his rifle and then finished off the last of the six attackers with his Colt .45.

Sgt Alvin York in 1919

York turned his attention back to the machine guns and was sharpshooting their gun crews like the turkeys he once hunted in the woods of Tennessee. During a brief lull in the firing, Leutnant Vollmer, concerned about the number of men York had already killed and for his wounded comrades, responded to York's demand for surrender by slowly standing up. York held his pistol to the officer's head as he ordered all enemy on the hill to surrender. They did, and York and his seven men brought 132 prisoners back to American lines.[37]

---

36   Whittlesey, McMurtry, and five others were awarded Medals of Honor. Whittlesey was also honored by being a pallbearer in the ceremony entombing the remains of the Unknown Soldier in Arlington National Cemetery. However, shattered by his wartime experiences, Whittlesey committed suicide in 1921. McMurtry, also a Wall Street lawyer like Whittlesey, died in 1958 at age 82.
In addition to the two airmen, Captain Nelson M Holderman, of Santa Anna, California, and First Sergeant Benjamin Kaufman, of Brooklyn, New York, were awarded Medals of Honor for heroism during the engagement. Cher Ami, the pigeon, is now stuffed and mounted in the Smithsonian Institution.

37   Alvin York, a farmer born in a two-room cabin in Pall Mall, Tennessee, third of eleven children, and who only had nine months of formal schooling, was promoted to sergeant and awarded the Medal of Honor, the French *Croix de Guerre* and *Legion of Honor*.
After the war York was offered thousands of dollars for public appearances or product

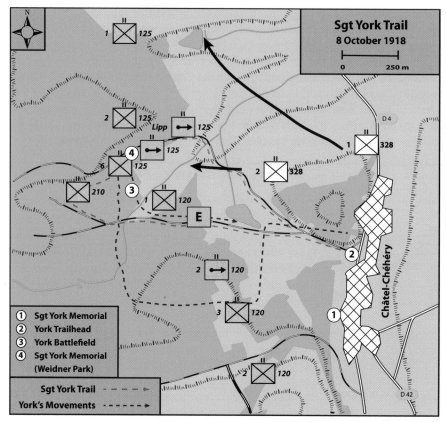

Sergeant York Battlefield

The 5-kilometer Sergeant York Discovery Trail (*Circuit du Sergeant Alvin York*) leads to the exact location where Corporal Alvin York fought off the famous bayonet attack and earned the Medal of Honor. The site holds a memorial stone honoring all seventeen Americans engaged in the actions on 8 October 1918 and an information board. Nine wooden signs mark points of interest along the loop trail. (49.286167, 4.934472)

Leave Châtel-Chéhéry north on highway D4 and follow into Fléville. Stop near the memorial at the intersection on the right. (49.305278, 4.969590)

The 1st Division entered the line at 05:30 on 1 October with the mission to drive a deep wedge into the high ground east of the Aire valley in preparation for an assault on the *Kriemhilde Stellung*. Amid dense use of gas shells and despite flanking fire, the assault battalion of the 16th Regiment cleared snipers and machine guns out of Ferme des Granges, crossed Exermont ravine, and entered Fléville on 4 October. The assault cost 18 of its 20 officers and 560 of its 800 men.

recommendations. He turned them all down promoting only charitable or civic causes. He returned to farming and hunting. York died in Nashville, Tennessee in 1964 at age 76.

The memorial is dedicated to the **16th Regiment, 1st Division** which liberated the village of Fléville on 4 October 1918. During this engagement, twenty-seven of the soldiers of the 16th Regiment were awarded the Distinguished Service Cross. The rough-edged stone bears a handsome plaque stating, in part, that after the liberation of Fléville, the 16th Regiment adopted the Blue and White Fur Vair shield from the town's Coat of Arms, as the background for its Regimental Crest.

16th Regiment Monument in Fléville

> Proceed north (D946) for 3.0 km to the memorial on the right at the junction with highway D54. (49.330015, 4.956782)

The 1st Division continued its drive north and east through some of the most heavily defended regions, including the powerful position known as the **Romagne Heights**. The 1st Infantry Division eagle commemorates the Meuse-Argonne battles where the division suffered 1,790 killed and 7,126 wounded. The plaque states, 'The 1st Division AEF attacked on the morning of October 4, 1918. In eight days of severe combat it forced the German line back 7 km and assisted the 1st American Army to join the French Fourth Army at Grandpré, thus driving the enemy from the Argonne.'

> Turn toward Romagne-sous-Montfaucon (D54, becomes D123).

The road traverses the area of the third German line, now with trees softening the contours of what were then sharp ridges. The strategic and strongly fortified **Côte de Châtillon**, 3 kilometers east of Sommerance and 1.5 kilometers to the north of the highway, was captured after extensive losses on 17 October by 84th Brigade, 42nd 'Rainbow' Division, commanded by Brigadier General Douglas MacArthur.

Near Landres-et-St-Georges on 14/15 October 1918 Lieutenant Colonel William Donovan, chief of staff of the 165th Regiment, led his unit into battle. The spirited Donovan ignored the officers' custom of covering insignia of rank (targets for snipers) and instead sallied forth wearing his medals boldly stating, 'They can't hit me, and they won't hit you!' Struck in the knee by a bullet, he refused to be evacuated and continued to direct his men until even American tanks were turning back under withering German fire. Donovan was awarded the Medal of Honor.[38]

---

38 Earlier in the war, Major Donovan, a prestigious Irish-American lawyer from Buffalo, New York, suffered a shrapnel wound in one leg and was almost blinded by gas. After performing a rescue under fire, he was offered the *Croix de Guerre*, but turned it down because a Jewish soldier who had taken part in the rescue had not also been awarded the honor. When this insult was corrected, Donovan accepted the distinction. He also was awarded the Distinguished Service Cross for leading

> In the village of Romagne the road intersects with highway D998; turn north and continue 250 m to the cemetery. (49.334204, 5.082335)

Romagne-sous-Montfaucon German Military Cemetery was begun in 1914 as a burial ground for nearby hospitals. Many of the dead resulted from fighting at the Butte de Vauquois and at the west bank of the Verdun battlefield. The main entrance consists of a small leafy glade leading through a red sandstone gatehouse which houses a chapel. The cemetery holds 1,412 burials identified by slate crosses under mature pine trees. Several interesting private and unit memorials can be found around its periphery.

> Return to highway D123 and continue east into the American cemetery. (49.334338, 5.093461)

Meuse-Argonne American Cemetery
Rue du Général Pershing, 55110 Romagne-sous-Montfaucon, France
Tel: +33 (0)3 29 85 14 18
See introduction for hours and web site.

The Meuse-Argonne Cemetery is the largest American military cemetery in Europe. Its location marks some of the most difficult fighting experienced by American troops in the war. The *Kriemhilde Stellung*, the strongest section of the Hindenburg Line, ran along the ridge behind the chapel. During the period of 9 to 13 October, five American divisions repeatedly attempted to dislodge the defenders, each time driven back by dense enemy fire. The villages of Cunel and Romagne were taken and lost several times. On 14 October, despite a two-hour enemy artillery bombardment upon its front trenches, the 5th Division fought through sweeping machine-gun fire from the Bois de Pultière north of Cunel and, by 11:00, captured the slopes upon which the cemetery rests. Unable to advance farther, they sheltered in shell craters near the current reflecting pool and awaited the night. The 32nd Division entered the village and held it despite an engulfing gas shell barrage during the night. The 5th Division continued its fight, requiring eight days to clear the enemy from the Bois des Rappes northeast of the cemetery. The seven American divisions suffered a total of 27,000 casualties in the vicinity of the cemetery, while cracking the Hindenburg Line.

The huge cemetery now contains 14,246 graves in eight plots. The painstakingly groomed grounds surround the Carrera marble markers which identify each grave. The Memorial Chapel at the far end of the cemetery and opposite the Visitor's Center offers a sanctuary for private reflection. Its stained-glass windows display the insignia of divisions of the American Expeditionary Force. The arcaded walls of the chapel list the names of 954 dead whose bodies were never found.

---

an assault during the Aisne-Marne campaign, in which hundreds of his regiment died, including his acting adjutant, poet Joyce Kilmer.

Widely traveled during the interwar years, Donovan established relationships with most world leaders. In July 1941 he formed America's first formal intelligence gathering service, the OSS (Office of Strategic Services) the forerunner of the CIA. Donovan died in 1959 at age 76 and is buried in Arlington National Cemetery.

Romagne-sous-Montfaucon

Arcade of the Missing, Meuse-Argonne American Cemetery, (right). German bunker and American grave, (below). NARA
US 4th Divsion Monument near Fismes, (below, right).

Consenvoye German Cemetery, (left).

US 316th Regiment Monument, (below).

US 5th Division Monument near Cunel, (left).

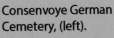

> Continue east into Cunel (D123) and stop near the east side of the church. (49.335568, 5.117110)

Cunel was the scene of many desperate conflicts between 9 and 14 October, in which the 80th, 3d and 5th Divisions participated. The town was captured several times but not held because it was dominated by German positions in the Bois de la Pultière to the north. The town and the wood, which was defended with the greatest tenacity, were finally captured on 14 October; by the 5th and 3rd Divisions respectively.

The east exterior wall of the village church holds a memorial commemorating three 'American Citizens' from Boston who died for liberty. Ensign Robert Fitzgerald Clark killed 21 August 1918 when his seaplane crashed into Brest Harbor, France; 2nd Lieutenant Charles Henry Fisk III former ambulance driver in the American Field Service who died in a Paris hospital of wounds received in July 1918 while with the 28th Division near Fismes; and 1st Lieutenant Aaron Davis Weld of the 3rd Division killed 11 October 1918.

> Proceed 550 m south on highway D15 to the monument. (49.329788, 5.119444)

The **5th Division** monument marks the jumping off trench for the 9th Infantry Brigade's attack of 14 October upon the *Kriemhilde Stellung* defenses and Romagne-sous-Montfaucon. The unit relieved the 80th Division and elements of the 4th Division that had fought through the Bois de Ogons on 11/12 October.

> Continue 1.3 km south passing through the Bois de Ogons before pausing at the large farm on the left. (49.318978, 5.121062)

Ferme de la Madeleine, marked by its red roof barn beside the highway, is at the southern edge of Bois des Ogons. The old building, formerly used by the Germans as a hospital, had been carefully prepared for defense and was the scene of desperate fighting from 28 September to 9 October. The first attacks by units of the 4th and 79th Divisions, supported by tanks, were repulsed on 28 September. Then the 3rd, 4th, 79th and 80th Divisions all engaged in bitter fighting in its vicinity. The battered ruins of the farm were finally captured by troops of the 3rd Division on 9 October.

The large Bois des Ogons to the northwest was entered by troops of the 4th and 79th Divisions on 28 September, but they were forced back by counterattacks. The following day elements of both divisions entered the wood but were again forced to fall back. The 80th Division attacked on 4 October making frontal and flank assaults without success until dark when the far edge was reached. Attempts to capture the entire wood by infiltration that night were unsuccessful. On 5 October, despite desperate efforts during the daytime, no progress could be made. About 18:00, however, the division again reached the far edge, which it outposted, and successfully organized a defensive position across the center of the wood.

Nantillois German Cemetery, along a side road immediately south of Madeleine Farm, holds 918 graves beneath solitary iron crosses. The burials resulted from intense local fighting. (49.318523, 5.125435)

> Continue 3.1 km into the center of Nantillois at the intersection of highways D15 and D164. (49.297956, 5.140011)

Nantillois was almost destroyed during the four-year German occupation. The 315th Regiment, 79th Division liberated the town on 28 September 1918. The 80th Division relieved the 79th Division on 30 September and suffered terrible losses in the attack on the Bois des Ogons and Madeleine Farm.

The **Nantillois Monument** is approached up a staircase and short stone walk. The center stone, once a fountain, is flanked by brick walls and inscribed 'This Monument has been erected by the State of PENNSYLVANIA' – in huge letters – 'a tribute to the heroic service and noble achievement of the 80th Division American Expeditionary Forces.'

Meuse-Argonne 1918
7 Grande Rue, 55270 Nantillois, France
Tel: +33 (0)329 861987
Email: meuse-argonne1918@hotmail.com
Open Thursday through Sunday from 12:00 to 18:00 1 May to 31 October.

A small private museum located within a B&B shows the German occupation of 1914-1918. The main interest is the Meuse-Argonne offensive with a collection of relics, dioramas, uniforms and weapons, including personal items and their stories. Organized battlefield walks can be arranged through the museum. (49.298662, 5.138170)

> Return to Cunel. A second 5th Division obelisk peeks above trimmed hedges north of Cunel alongside highway D15 toward Bantheville to identify the northern limit of the unit's attack. (49.35202 5.09954)
> Continue east toward Brieulles-sur-Meuse (D123).

The **Brieulles German Military Cemetery** is signed from the center of town and is found up a short dirt track to the north. The cemetery holds 11,277 German soldiers in single and mass graves as it rolls up the hill from the entrance. At the top of the hill an eight-tier mass grave is topped by a large white stone cross. Visitors are rewarded with views down upon the Meuse River and of the heights across the river that sheltered German gun emplacements and gave the Americans such a hard time. (49.339854, 5.180756)

> In Brieulles turn left toward Dun-sur-Meuse (D164) noting the white stone stele with a red diamond 220 m south of the intersection. (49.335546, 5.186536)

On 1 November 1918 the American First Army began the final push. The 5th Division was given the task to cross the river at Cléry-le-Petit. At 16:20 on 4 November, 2nd Battalion, 60th Regiment and 2nd Battalion, 61st Regiment reached the banks of the river.

On 4 November, 6th Regiment, 10th Brigade forced passage of the Meuse and its canal opposite this point to become the first Allied troops to cross the Meuse. During the night of 3/4 November Company F, 7th Engineers, 5th Division threw foot bridges across Meuse and its canal for assaulting infantry. Simultaneously with passage of assault battalions, Companies A and C, 7th Engineers, threw a heavy pontoon bridge across Meuse and canal on the night of 4/5 November.

> Continue north on highway D164 for 3.3 km to the stele beside the highway. (49.365102, 5.181021)

Company A, 7th Engineer Regiment started work on the first footbridge by carrying their pontoon boats across 1,500 meters of open ground. At this moment a tremendous fire of machine guns and artillery burst on the exposed troops. The infantry sought shelter, but the engineers bravely continued at their work. Shells sank their boats as fast as they could be placed in the water and by 18:00 no boats were left.

Company D repeated the effort a short distance to the south during the night. At one point German artillery destroyed three pontoon boats, engineers jumped into the icy river and held up the deck of the bridge until replacement pontoons could be

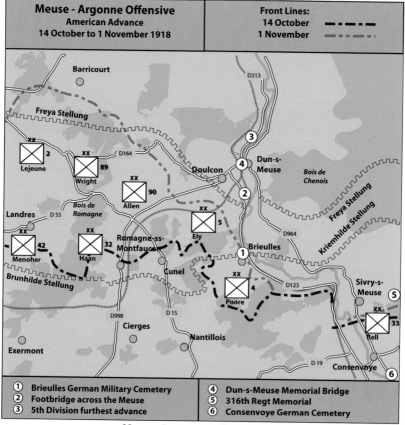

Meuse-Argonne Offensive Phase 3

launched and installed. The first infantry company crossed the river and two canal bridges by 05:00 the next morning.[39]

The white stone stele with the **5th Division's red diamond** emblem marks the location to the east where the initial footbridge was constructed.

Continue to junction with highway D998 in Doulcon. Another **5th Division stele** with red diamond stands almost lost behind dense shrubs behind the local war memorial in the intersection. Two kilometers to the north upon the roadside embankment above the highway another stele bearing the **5th Division**'s red diamond marks the furthest advance of the division during the war. (49.39605 5.17456)

Follow highway D998 east into Dun-sur-Meuse and the bridges crossing the three arms of the Meuse River. Note the metal railing on the third bridge. (49.385281, 5.182819)

5th Division railing on the bridge over the Meuse River in Dun-sur-Meuse

The nested metal plates commemorate (in French and English) the **5th Division** crossing of the Meuse stating, 'The Veterans of the 5th Division American Expeditionary Force have erected this railing to commemorate the crossing of the Meuse River and the establishment of a bridgehead on its eastern bank by their division during the World War.'

Turn right toward Verdun (D964); after 210 m note the beautifully detailed Mairie on the left. Inside a memorial, dedicated to the 6th Engineers, 3rd Division, commemorates the sacrifice of Captain Charles Dashiell Harris, commander of the 6th Engineers who was mortally wounded on 20 October while clearing a German machine gun nest in the Clairs Chênes Woods. (49.384063, 5.184724) Continue 300 m to the marker on the right. (49.385281, 5.182819)

The white concrete stele bears the red diamond insignia of the **5th Division** and three granite plaques. The first plaque commemorates the liberation of Dun-sur-Meuse by the 5th Division on 5 November 1918 and Major AN Stark, Jr, a unit officer. The second plaque commemorates the reinforcing of the pontoon bridge used by the 5th Division during the Meuse-Argonne Offensive by the 7th Engineers. The third, diamond-shaped plaque honors the 14th Machine Gun Battalion, which was attached to the 9th Brigade during the Meuse-Argonne Offensive.

---

39   Including their commander, Major William Hoge, who had reconnoitered the site that afternoon while under enemy artillery and machine-gun fire, engineers Sergeant Eugene P Walker, Corporal Robert E Crawford and Privates Noah L Gump, John Hoggle and Stanley T Murmane all were awarded Distinguished Service Crosses for their heroic actions.

> Continue south along the Meuse River toward Verdun (D964).

North of Consenvoye, the road goes up the shoulder of the ridge east of the Meuse and offers tremendous views of the river below and the field and forest dotted landscape on the western bank. This is the eastern edge of the American attack zone of the Meuse-Argonne Battlefield. After crossing a crest in the road, the village of Sivry-sur-Meuse appears in the valley below with a beautiful profile of its church's two towers.

Sivry-sur-Meuse had been occupied since September 1914 and, ironically, became the site of one of the last battles of the war. An airfield was built on the flats between the canal and the Meuse. German pilots, notably including Oswald Boelcke and Baron Manfred von Richthofen, fought French squadrons and the Escadrille La Fayette in the skies above. On 28 October the village was bombarded from the heights of Dannevoux to the west and from Consenvoye to the south. In early November, an infantry attack left little of the village intact.

A private monument dedicated to the **316th Regiment, 79th Division** is located above Sivry-sur-Meuse on a height named La Grande Montagne (Hill 378) that held a German stronghold. The 10-meter-high granite tower is visible against the horizon from the Meuse River road (D964). Hill 378 was captured by French troops, but the American regiment chose this site for its memorial, against the expressed wishes of General Pershing, because the height is equidistant between Montfaucon and the regiment's later battlefields to the east. The memorial can be accessed by highway C1, one-lane, two-direction road that passes through the Forêt de Sivry and along the shoulder of this high ground.

> Continue to the German Cemetery 1.1 km south of the village of Consenvoye. (49.279750, 5.296493)

Consenvoye German Cemetery is fronted by a red sandstone wall with a gate providing entrance onto a small red sandstone portico. The cemetery holds 11,146 German soldiers, 63 Austro-Hungarian soldiers, one Russian and a German nursing nun. The mass grave across the rear of the cemetery is covered with low growing shrubs and groups of dark gray stone Crosses Pattée scattered randomly amongst the shrubs. The names of its 2,537 German soldiers are listed on a series of metal panels except for the 933 that were never identified. The cemetery commemorates a meeting on 22 September 1984 between French President François Mitterand and German Chancellor Helmut Kohl. The two leaders symbolically shook hands to signify the end of Franco-German conflict that had devastated Europe for the previous 114 years.

> Return to Consenvoye. Proceed east 17 km to enter the bleak farming village of Chaumont-devant-Damvillers and proceed to the church. Turn right and continue north on an unnamed road up the hillside to the large roadside stone marker. (49.30844, 5.42493)

Twenty-three-year-old Henry Gunther was of German-American heritage from Baltimore. Gunther, a member of Company A, 313th Regiment, had risen to the rank of sergeant and was responsible for his unit's supplies. He had written a letter home complaining about miserable conditions in the front line. Army censors intercepted the letter and Gunther was demoted to private.

On November 11th, Gunther was on patrol near Chaumont-devant-Damvillers when his unit approached a German roadblock. Soldiers of both armies had been fully informed of the war's end at 11:00. Gunther, reportedly obsessed with a determination to prove himself before his officers and fellow soldiers, rose and charged the German position despite his comrades and the German soldiers waving him back. Gunther fired a shot or two. When he got too close, the machine gun cut him down at 10:59 – one minute before the Armistice was to take effect. Henry Nicholas Gunther became the last soldier of any nationality to be killed during the First World War. He was restored to rank of sergeant – posthumously.

A **memorial stone** bears a stylized French flag and a few words (in French) 'In honor of Henry Gunther.' The stone marks the spot where Gunther was killed.

Armistice and Peace

After the failures of the *Kaiserschlacht* Offensives, Ludendorff knew that the war was lost. As early as 28 September, he had shared his opinion with Field Marshal Hindenburg, who had come to the same conclusion. Pressured by allied offensives along the Western Front and by the defeat of its Austrian, Turkish, and Bulgarian partners on other fronts, the German people were increasingly defeatist. Changes to the German government were instituted to make negotiations with United States President Woodrow Wilson more palatable by reducing governmental control by the military and the Kaiser. The military accepted the new civilian government's truce to preserve the 'honor' of the German Army while seeking an armistice that would preserve what remained of the army in exchange for territorial concessions. The new Chancellor, Prince Maximilian von Baden, initially refused to be the army's scapegoat, but eventually relented. Maximilian accepted a meeting conditioned upon President Wilson's Fourteen Points. Believing that the American conditions did not sufficiently punish the German people, French President Georges Clemenceau and British Prime Minister David Lloyd George protested that Wilson was negotiating behind their backs. Wilson backed off, fearing a German attempt to split the Allies.

Faced with the dissolution of his armies, renewed allied offensives, and the lack of support from the now independent-minded civilian government, Ludendorff resigned on 26 October. Meanwhile, the allied Supreme War Council, headed by Foch, met in Versailles to establish the military's armistice conditions.

In the first week of November, German deserters marched in protest in Berlin and Bolshevik elements in the German Navy seized several naval bases. Workers' councils seized the main Rhine bridges and stopped the flow of men and supplies. At 05:00 on 10 November, Kaiser Wilhelm II left the Supreme Command Headquarters at Spa, Belgium to go into exile in neutral Holland. His abdication became official on 28 November 1918, ending the 250-year Hohenzollern Dynasty.

Rethondes Clairière de l'Armistice
8 to 11 November 1918

REPRESENTATIVES	
FRENCH:	Supreme Allied Commander maréchal Ferdinand Foch
BRITISH:	First Lord of the British Admiralty Admiral Rosslyn Wemyss
GERMAN:	Secretary of State Matthias Erzberger
RESULT	The Germans signed the armistice declaration, ending hostilities pending negotiation of the Treaty of Versailles.
LOCATION	Compiègne is 80 km north of Paris; the Forest of Rethondes is 7 km east of Compiègne

Events

On 7 November, the German delegation, led by Secretary of State Matthias Erzberger, a centrist politician, left the Kaiser's headquarters at Spa by motorcar. Generalmajor Detlev von Winterfeldt, the son of the man who had dictated the terms of France's surrender in 1870 and a former military attaché in Paris, was the army's representative. Field Marshall Hindenburg and members of the German General Staff declined participation. Upon leaving Spa, Chancellor Prince Baden begged Erzberger to secure peace. The pressure on Erzberger was tremendous and, in addition, his son had died of influenza three weeks earlier. After a circuitous route through recent battlefields, the delegation arrived at the forest clearing at 05:30 the next morning.

Waiting for them was Supreme Allied Commander maréchal Ferdinand Foch, Chief of Staff général de division Maxime Weygand, and First Lord of the British Admiralty Admiral Rosslyn Wemyss, who had arrived earlier that morning. No Americans were present. Foch's demands were non-negotiable and were to be accepted as presented. The German delegation remained in the clearing for three days while negotiations with authorities in Berlin took place. At 02:05 on 11 November, the new civilian government of Chancellor Friedrick Ebert in Berlin replied that they agreed. At 05:05, Erzberger signed the document on behalf of the German Government. The armistice took effect at 11:00 that morning. The guns finally fell silent.

Aftermath

With armistice declared, the German army demobilized; tired, sick, and disillusioned men walked home. Prince Max handed the Chancellorship to Fritz Ebert, an ex-cobbler and Social Democrat. President Wilson arrived in France on 14 December 1918 to participate in the Peace Conference held at the Palace of Versailles near Paris. Only the victors were present because political events in Germany transformed a military armistice into unconditional surrender. Wilson's Fourteen Points were again ignored while Clemenceau, Lloyd George, and Italian Premier Vittorio Emanuele Orlando imposed punishing economic terms on Germany. Great Britain wanted to expand its Colonial Empire; France wanted a Germany on its knees and guarantees against future aggression; Italy – late to empire building – wanted overseas colonies. Wilson sacrificed his Fourteen Points in return for establishing collective security through the League of Nations. The leaders produced a document that was punitive and unworkable, filled with territorial contradictions. German Foreign Minister Count Brockdorff-Rantzau was appalled at the conditions when he arrived and initially refused to accept it. The allied blockade of German ports, however, was still in existence, and the German population was on the verge of starvation. On 28 June 1919, the Treaty of Versailles was signed in the same Hall of Mirrors where the German Empire had been created only 48 years earlier. Wilson returned to the United States ill and disillusioned. Thirteen and one-half years later, Adolf Hitler, the enemy the treaty had helped to create, was elected Chancellor of Germany.

Consequences of the War

In the decades after the First World War, recriminations abounded as to who was at fault for starting the great conflagration. Some historians believe that a system of alliances and predetermined army mobilization schedules forced the parties into fighting. The 'winners' blamed the 'losers' intransigence and militarism, but with over 20 million dead blame lies on both sides.

The war ended the dynastic houses of middle Europe that had ruled for centuries. The monarchical governments of Austria, Germany, and Russia were all replaced. The Ottoman Empire in Turkey disappeared. Like the Congress of Vienna at the end of the Napoleonic era, the Paris Conference redrew the political map of Europe, attempting to re-establish the balance of power. Germany lost industrialized Silesia, parts of Pomerania and West Prussia, and the Danzig Corridor to a reformed Poland. Alsace and Lorraine were returned to France. Minor adjustments were made to the borders with Belgium and Denmark. Germany's African colonies were occupied by Britain, and its Pacific Islands went under a Japanese Mandate from the League of Nations.

The human consequences of the war are the casualty totals. On the Western Front, France suffered the most, with 1,385,300 dead or missing – 10 per cent of its male working population and 27 per cent of men between the ages of 18 and 27. It would take 35 years for the country to regain its prewar population level. British Armies had 908,500 dead – 750,000 on the Western front – including 56,625 Canadians and 59,000 Australians. America's losses were significantly smaller in keeping with its late entry but were still a substantial 116,750 dead; 85,000 fell on the Western Front, of which 52,947 were battle deaths. Belgium, with its much smaller population, lost 40,367. Italy's losses in its Alpine battles against Austro-Hungary were a staggering 460,000. Totals for all allied armies on the Western Front were 2.3 million dead. Russian military deaths were estimated at 1,700,000, but an accurate number is impossible to determine.

German casualty figures were accurately tabulated until the army dissolved in the last months of the war. German losses for all fronts for the entire war were 1,718,250. To this day 768,000 German soldiers remain buried in military cemeteries in France. Germany's allies added 1,200,000 from Austria-Hungary, 335,750 from Turkey and 101,250 from Bulgaria to the death toll.

In total, the fighting resulted in 8.2 million dead, 7 million disabled, and 12 million carrying the physical or psychological scars of combat. Those classified as prisoners (many of whom returned) or missing (many of whom did not) totaled 7.5 million, of which a large percentage occurred on the Eastern Front. Western Europe added an additional 5 million civilian casualties, not including the effects of the influenza pandemic, which are estimated at 27 million deaths.

The monetary cost of the war has been estimated to be as high as $250 billion at today's valuation. Agricultural production and industrial output of the ravaged participants remained below prewar levels for a decade. France had 250,000 buildings destroyed and almost 10,000 square miles of land laid waste. Britain lost approximately 10 million tons of shipping to German submarine warfare. At the end one side thought that it had won, but in reality both sides had lost.

Tour

Although not a battlefield, the significance of Rethondes Clairière de l'Armistice to the two world wars and the colorful nature of the events that occurred here warrant a visit and this special tour section.

The forest of Compiègne is a lowland area bordered by the Oise and Aisne Rivers. The boggy woods are confined by a series of hills running from north to east to south. Once a favorite playground of French kings, approximately 1,500 kilometers

Rethondes Clairière de l'Armistice

Alsace-Lorraine Monument in the Rethondes Armistice Clearing, (right).

Mémorial du Wagon de l'Armistice, (below).

Armistice Clearing: the bollards mark the locations of the French and German railcars, (below). Note: maréchal Ferdinand Foch's statue in the center, rear.

of roads, horse trails, and footpaths remain through the beech and oak groves. Just outside its borders are Château Pierrefonds, the famous residence of Napoleon III, and the early Gothic, 12th century church at Morienvald. The site is a popular tourist destination because of its historical significance and proximity to Paris. The city and forest offer numerous cultural, historic, and natural destinations.

> Leave Compiègne east on avenue de l'Armistice (N31) to enter the Forêt de Rethondes. Continue straight on highway D546 and proceed directly to the Armistice Clearing parking area. (49.428976, 2.907711)

A significant cause of France's going to war in 1914 was the return of the provinces of Alsace and Lorraine that Germany had annexed after the Franco-Prussian War in 1871. The **Alsace-Lorraine Monument** at the roundabout before the parking area commemorates the sacrifices of all French soldiers who fought for the return of those regions. A block arch of Alsatian sandstone stands over a sword, which is stabbing a prostrate German Imperial eagle. Inscribed in the top of the arch is the date 11 November 1918. Across the front of the stone platform are the words 'To the heroic soldiers of France – defenders of fatherland and right – glorious liberators of Alsace and Lorraine.' The monument so infuriated Adolf Hitler that in 1940 he had it destroyed, and the pieces shipped to Germany. It was found and reconstructed after the Second World War. (49.429370, 2.905777)

During the war the **Armistice Clearing** was a boggy wood containing a network of rail lines used for heavy artillery installations bombarding the German lines 20 kilometers away. The guns were cleared away to make room for maréchal Foch's private rail car on one side and that of the German representatives on the other. The two trains parked no more than 100 meters apart. Short sections of track remain and memorial granite slabs resembling sarcophagi mark the spots where the cars stood. A stone terrace between the two cars' locations commemorates the event with the words, 'Here on 11 November 1918 succumbed the criminal pride of the German Empire. Vanquished by the free peoples it sought to enslave.' Those powerful words fully represented the feelings of the allied peoples, who had fought the war since 1914 and who had suffered so terribly during four years of conflict, fear, and deprivation. In 1940, Hitler had the slabs broken up and shipped to Berlin. The entire clearing was demolished, trees were cut down, and the earth was plowed over to remove any trace of Germany's humiliation. Compiègne was liberated on 1 September 1944, and the local population immediately forced German PoWs to restore the clearing. The terrace blocks were recovered and reassembled. (49.427288, 2.906476) Since 1937, a statue of maréchal Foch has looked over the site from among tall evergreen shrubs at the edge of the clearing. In respect for the French military leader, the statue was not damaged by the German occupiers. (49.427437, 2.907236)

Mémorial du Wagon de l'Armistice
Route de Soissons, 60200 Compiègne, France
Tel/fax: +33 (0)3 44 85 14 18
Email: wagon.armistice@wanadoo.fr
Web: http://www.musee-armistice-14-18.fr/

Open daily, except Tuesdays, October through March from 09:00 to 12:00 and 14:00 to 17:30; April through September until 18:30; afternoons only in December and January.

Wagon Lits Company coach #2419D was originally a dining car. In 1918, it serviced maréchal Foch as a traveling office and accommodation. After the momentous signing of the Armistice within its walls, the coach returned to regular service, but quickly became a popular attraction when installed in Les Invalides in Paris. In 1927, it was installed in a specially constructed museum at the edge of the clearing.

During the Second World War, Hitler ordered that Foch's rail car be removed from the museum and replaced in its 1918 location. On 22 June 1940, to the great glee of Hitler and his entourage, the French delegation, led by the aging maréchal Henri Pétain, was presented terms there by the German military and France formally surrendered. The rail car was transported to Berlin as a trophy to be mounted in a new museum that was never built. After being briefly displayed at the Brandenburg Gate, it was housed in Anhalt Station until allied bombing raids on Berlin threatened its survival. Hidden in the forest at Orhdurf, Thuringia, 280 kilometers southeast of Berlin, SS troops destroyed it in the closing days of the war.

A revised museum was constructed in 1950 which houses a replacement rail car of similar vintage as coach #2419D. A room displays artifacts from both the 1918 armistice and the 1940 surrender. Newspapers, documents, photographs, and the seating arrangements for the signing are included. Original documents from the First World War were hidden at the outbreak of the second war and later returned to the coach. An audio presentation describes the events. (49.426917, 2.905744)

Paris Tour Sites

France's capital offers opportunity to review numerous sites that describe or commemorate events in the country's military history. In particular, three of those sites are dedicated to America's participation in the war.

France's premier military museum is in Paris' 7th arrondisement 1.4 km southeast of the Eifel Tower. (48.855837, 2.312610)

Musée de l'Armée
129 Rue de Grenelle, 75007 Paris, France
Tel: +33 (0)8 10 11 33 99
Web: http:/www.musee-armee.fr/

Open daily 1 April to 31 October from 10:00 to 18:00; 1 November to 31 March: from 10:00 to 17:00. Admission fee. The Paris Museum Pass offers unlimited queue-jump access to all areas of the Musée de l'Armée, as well as over 60 other museums' permanent collections and monuments in Paris and the region.

L'Institution Nationale des Invalides was commissioned in 1670 by King Louis XIV as a hospital and home for ill or aged career soldiers — a function which it retains. The building's armory was the source of weapons used in the storming of the Bastille, the event that triggered the French revolution, on 14 July 1789. Napoleon I, members of his family, and many of France's most notable military figures are buried in the Dôme des Invalides. As the need for hospital space declined, army weapons museums were moved into the structure and the Musée de l'Armée was established in 1905.

As one approaches the complex from the north, cannon mounted on cast iron carriages and divided into two symmetrical groups line what once was the northern moat of Les Invalides forming the Triumphal Battery. Les Invalides' Main Courtyard holds a larger collection of French artillery pieces.

The Musée de l'Armée holds one of the largest collections of military artifacts in the world. The Old Department includes weapons and armor from the 13th century to the early 17th century. The Modern Department holds weapons and maps of the Thirty Years War, displays from the Revolution, Age of Napoleon, Crimean War, and colorful uniformed manikins from the Franco-Prussian War. The Contemporary Department has seven rooms identifying significant periods from the two world wars with the Second World War rooms having undergone a recent updating and refurbishment.

Place Charles de Gaulle is 2.6 km to the northwest. (48.873781, 2.295013)

L'Arc de Triomphe de l'Étoile stands at the western end of the Champs-Élysées in the center of Place Charles de Gaulle, formerly named Place de l'Étoile — the étoile or 'star' formed by the junction of twelve magnificent radiating avenues. The triumphant memorial was commissioned by Napoleon in 1806 after his victory at the Battle of Austerlitz, but construction was halted after the emperor's fall to be finally completed in 1836. Six reliefs are sculpted on the façades of the arch representing important moments during the French Revolution and the Napoleonic era.

The magnificent archway has witnessed marching conquering armies since its construction including the Germans after the Franco-Prussian War in 1871, the French Army in 1919, the victorious German Army in 1940, and the liberating Allied forces in 1944. An Unknown Soldier was entombed under the arch on Armistice Day, 1920 and an eternal flame lit. The tomb has since become the focal point for military commemorations large and small.

A memorial to American volunteers is in an expansive park 850 m south of the Arc de Triomphe. (48.868174, 2.293568)

American Volunteer Monument
Thomas Jefferson Park, Place des États-Unis, 75116 Paris, France
The statue upon a raised plinth honors Americans who volunteered to serve in French units. Paid for by private subscription, it memorializes the names of twenty-four citizens of the United States who fell in that service. The bronze statue is that of American poet Alan Seeger whose verse is inscribed on the base. He was killed in action July 4, 1916, a volunteer with the French Foreign Legion. [40]

The Suresnes American Cemetery is 7 km west of the Arc de Triomphe in the western suburb of Suresnes. (48.871971, 2.218814)

Suresnes American Cemetery
123 Boulevard Washington, 92150 Suresnes, France
Tel: +33 (0)1 46 25 01 70
See introduction for hours and website.
Originally a First World War cemetery for 1,541 Americans most of whom died in Parisian hospitals, the Suresnes American Cemetery and Memorial now also shelters twenty-four unknown dead from the Second World War in a separate grave plot. Consequently, the First World War Memorial Chapel was enlarged by the addition of two loggias that terminate in rooms holding white marble figures in memory of those who lost their lives in the two wars. The walls of the two loggias bear bas-reliefs of soldiers bearing the empty bier or shrouded remains of a dead comrade. In addition, bronze tablets on the walls of the chapel record the names of 974 missing soldiers who have no known grave.

The Lafayette Escadrille Memorial is 6 km southwest of the Suresnes American Cemetery on the grounds of the Domaine National de Ste-Cloud, a 19th century imperial residence in Marnes-la-Coquette. The Autoroute cuts through the domain, separating the Lafayette Memorial from other attractions in the domaine. A stark entrance gate provides the only access to the memorial. (Entrance gate: 48.871971, 2.218814; Memorial: 48.836674, 2.172449)

---

40   Alan Seeger was the uncle of American folk singer Pete Seeger, and was a classmate of TS Eliot at Harvard University. He wrote the poem *I Have a Rendezvous with Death*, a favorite of President John F. Kennedy.

Les Invalides and Arc de Triomphe

Hôtel National des Invalides complex with the Dôme des Invalides, (above).

Arc de Triomphe de l'Étoile, (below).

Arc de Triomphe and Suresnes American Cemetery

Arc de Triomphe reliefs: Departure of the Volunteers of 1792, also called La Marseillaise, (right) and the Funeral of General Marceau, a French general of The Revolution, (below).

The Arc de Triomphe's Tomb of the Unknown and its Eternal Flame, (left).

Suresnes American Cemetery, final resting place for 1,541 American war dead, (right).

Crypt de la Memorial Lafayette
9 Rue Yves Cariou,
92430 Marnes-la-Coquette

Lafayette Escadrille Memorial. (ABMC)

Open daily from 07:30 to 20:00 November through February; 07:30 to 21:00 during September, October, March, and April; and 07:30 to 22:00 May through August. Contact the Suresnes American Cemetery for availability of Crypt tours.

Americans sympathetic to the Allied cause offered their service to France as ambulance drivers and soldiers in the French Foreign Legion. By 1915, many of these volunteers began to lobby the French government to create an aero squadron composed of American pilots. After careful deliberation the French agreed, and on 20 April 1916 the first unit of American fliers was placed on frontline duty. These aviators fought in the Battle of Verdun and the Somme Offensive establishing a reputation for their daring and skill.

Although only thirty-eight were officially assigned to the Lafayette *Escadrille*, all two hundred Americans in the French Air Service, known as the *Service Aéronautique,* were considered to be part of the unofficial Lafayette Flying Corps. Many of these aviators transferred to American squadrons once America entered the war.

The Lafayette Escadrille Memorial Cemetery commemorates the birthplace of American combat aviation, and honors the American volunteer pilots who flew with French squadrons. It is the final resting place for some of America's first combat aviators and their French Officers. The monument is composed of a central arch, one-half size of the Arc de Triomphe in Paris. The central arch is flanked by wings on either side that include open hallways that terminate in pavilions. Upon the stones of the arc are inscribed the names of the dead American pilots of the Lafayette Escadrille and the Lafayette Flying Corps. Also inscribed are the names of the French towns and provinces where these pilots were involved in combat. A reflecting pool runs the length of the structure. A semi-circular terrace behind the memorial forms the roof of the crypt below. Thirteen stained-glass windows in the crypt depict the major battles of the Western Front and allow natural light to enter. The crypt holds sixty-eight sarcophagi although seventeen are symbolically empty because of difficulties in locating or removing the pilots' remains and two hold their French officers.

Versailles is 22 km southwest of Paris and can be easily reached by car or, preferably, the RER train system. Proceed to the chateau. (48.804851, 2.120345)

Château de Versailles
Place d'Armes, 78000 Versailles, France
Tel: + 33 (0)1 30 83 78 00
Web: http://en.chateauversailles.fr/
    The palace is open daily except Mondays and the gardens are open every day; hours of operation for the various sites on the grounds and buildings vary; please consult their website or any local tourist office.
    The palace of Versailles was constructed as a simple hunting lodge in 1624 by King Louis XIII. Future kings greatly expanded and enhanced the site. King Louis XIV established his royal residence there in 1682 and the site became known for its grandeur and opulence. The palace remained the principle residence of the kings of France until the French Revolution in 1789. The palace witnessed the signing of treaties that recognized the independence of the United States from Great Britain and ended the American Revolution in 1783, the unification Germany and establishment of the Second German Empire in 1871, and the Peace Treaty ending the First World War in 1919.
    The Château de Versailles is now a major tourist attraction and UNESCO World Heritage site for its expansive gardens, elaborate fountains, ornate state and private apartments, and secluded pavilions. The 73-meter-long Hall of Mirrors is literally that with 357 mirrors spread across 17 arches. The signing of the Treaty of Versailles ending the war occurred in the hall on 28 June 1919.

Index

V

W

Y